Treasures in Heaven

Various

ISBN: 978-1-61895-193-9

PREFACE

No lesson taught by the Savior during his ministry in mortality was more frequently and thoroughly impressed than that of unselfish service. Of those who labored solely for the things of this world, or for praise or the honors that men can bestow, He had a habit of saying: "They have their reward." If they obtained that which they strove for they were already repaid: they were entitled to nothing more. Of the rich He said, "Ye have received your consolation." It was not sufficient that man should seek to benefit or bring happiness alone to those they loved. Even that He evidently regarded as a species of selfishness, as implied by the saying: "For if ye love them which love you, what reward have ye?" "For sinners do even the same." His exhortation was: "Lay not up for yourselves treasures upon earth, where moth and rust doth corrupt, and where thieves break through and steal; but lay up for yourselves treasures in heaven, where neither moth nor rust doth corrupt, and where thieves do not break through nor steal."

All this was not intended to imply that wealth itself was intrinsically bad, or that poverty had any essential virtue, except as a means to an end. The rule was, as expressed by the great Teacher, that "where the treasure is, there will the heart be also." A sublime test upon this point was that made of the young man who applied to the Savior upon one occasion to know what good thing he could do to gain eternal life. Though he was able to say that he had kept all the commandments from his youth up, it was apparent to the Master that his heart was set upon the wealth he possessed, as evidence of which he turned away sorrowfully when required by the Savior to surrender his possessions, for the benefit of the poor, and follow Him.

The Gospel as revealed anew in our day has shed a flood of light upon the subject of salvation, and the conditions upon which it is predicated. The glorious principle of salvation for the dead, as revealed through the Prophet Joseph Smith, has awakened a desire in the hearts of thousands of earnest seekers after truth to do a vicarious work for the benefit of their dead relatives and friends, that they may share in all the blessings and privileges of the Gospel. In this work, as well as in the preaching of the Gospel to the living, have avenues been opened up for unselfish work, which, as it involves no earthly reward, is clearly in the line of laying up treasures in heaven, as distinguished from the work of amassing treasures upon earth which absorbs the attention of so many of the earth's inhabitants. That the recital of some typical examples of sacrifices unselfishly made in the interest of others, and th—e joy experienced therein, may tend to promote faith in those who read the same and incite them also to lay up treasures in heaven, this volume is published in continuation of the "Faith Promoting Series," originated and published by the present author about thirty-five years ago.

CONTENTS

CHAPTER I

CHAPTER II

CHAPTER III

CHAPTER IV

CHAPTER V

CHAPTER VI

CHAPTER VII

CHAPTER VIII

A WOMAN WITH A PURPOSE

AN EXCEPTION

MY MOTHER

CHAPTER I

CHAPTER II

EXAMPLES OF RIGHTEOUS ZEAL

CHAPTER I

BIRTH OF NIELS—OBSCURE CHILDHOOD—CRIPPLED, HELPLESS CONDITION—GOSPEL PREACHED—TAUGHT NEEDLEWORK—TRAINING IN BIBLE AND LUTHERAN CREED—A PROPHETIC PRIEST—REMARKABLE PREDICTION CONCERNING NIELS.

Perhaps no better example of unselfish service in the interest of others, of patience and forbearance under the burden of a serious physical handicap and courage and persistence in a labor of love and sacrifice can be found than is afforded in the life of the hero whose portrait is herewith presented.

Niels P. L. Eskildz was born May 31, 1836, at Lindholm, County of Aalborg, Denmark, only a few miles from the city of Aalborg, which is celebrated as being the birthplace of President Anthon H. Lund. The parents of Niels were unassuming, country folks, with nothing to distinguish them from their industrious and respectable neighbors except their rather unusual size and a certain pride of bearing and correctness of speech, due to their superior education, and the fact that they were both descendants in a direct line from noble, titled families.

They had a small farm, the cultivation of which furnished them little more than a modest living, and the father combined the occupation of butcher with that of farmer, by slaughtering animals and selling meat in the village market place every Wednesday and Saturday.

Niels was the youngest of the family, having two brothers of almost gigantic stature and a sister who, when grown, was the largest woman in that part of Denmark. Niels also, would doubtless have grown to be an unusually large man had he not met with an awful accident when ten years of age.

Denmark is a country almost without fences, the farms being

separated one from another by imaginary lines. Instead of the cows and sheep owned by the farmers being allowed to range at will in pastures, the custom was and still is to stake them out individually, and lead them in at night. As a rule the cows are models of decorum, and one of the prettiest as well as commonest sights of the country is to see a boy or girl marching a number of cows, like so many soldiers, in double file and close rank from the pasture to the barn.

Niels, having been sent by his parents to thus bring a cow in from the field, the creature, though usually docile, suddenly became fractious and, running around the boy, tangled him up in the rope, and then frantically dragged him through a grain field and against numerous obstructions before she could be stopped. When released the poor boy was found to have a broken thigh and other serious injuries, from the effects of which he was bedfast for more than three years. It was feared he never would recover, but his patient mother gave him the most devoted attention and relieved the tedium of his helplessness by teaching him needlework, at which she was an adept, and by reading to him. In course on time he grew strong enough to be propped up in a chair and thus carried into the open air, but the exertion was probably too much for him, as he soon had a relapse, and during the ensuing two years spent most of his time in bed. His spine by degrees became so curved and deformed that, while his legs were nearly of normal length, his body had the appearance of having been crumpled down thereon, and his large, well-shaped head crowded down between his shoulders.

In the year 1850 Apostle Erastus Snow arrived in Denmark as a missionary. He had not been there long when the Gospel influence began to be felt and converts to flock to his standard. One family among the residents of Lindholm embraced the Gospel, and soon found themselves somewhat notorious because of the attention they received from the local Lutheran priest, near whose chapel the family lived, and his frequent public comments on their abandonment of the Lutheran faith and acceptance of the unpopular doctrines of "Mormonism."

In those days the Lutheran church held almost undisputed sway throughout Denmark, and the invariable rule was for children to be diligently taught the Bible and drilled in a knowledge of the Lutheran creed from their infancy. When the children attain the age of about thirteen years they are required to appear before the priest for a series of examinations, as to their knowledge of these subjects before being confirmed as members of the Lutheran church.

When Niels was fourteen years old, and was barely able to hobble about a little on crutches, he was cited to appear with a class of dozen or more children before the priest, to be catechised. This they did many times until they were able to answer satisfactorily all the questions propounded to them. At about the first of these meetings a young girl asked to be excused from the examinations, because her parents had joined the "Mormons," and she expected to. She cited in support of her plea, that the King of Denmark had granted religious liberty. Her request was complied with by the priest, who proceeded to comment on "Mormonism" then and at every subsequent meeting in a way that indicated that he must have been studying "Mormon" literature, and Niels very strongly suspected that the priest was really converted to "Mormonism," although he either lacked the courage to embrace it, or considered it impolitic to do so. Whether this surmise was correct or not, the priest seemed to have "Mormonism" constantly in his mind, and his frequent allusions to its doctrines and the scripture supporting the same had the effect of converting Niels to "Mormonism." Though he did not then declare his belief in the Gospel, he had not from that time a doubt of its truth.

That priest, whose name was Holger Christopher Kongslev Thryde, was a very peculiar man, a thorough scriptorian, a keen reasoner and withal quite inspirational. When the class of which Niels was a member had received sufficient training by him to appear for public examination and confirmation as members of the Lutheran church, they were all notified to be present at the regular Sunday service in the chapel. There they were separately catechised by the priest in presence of the congregation. Their answers being satisfactory, he asked each in turn as to his willingness to enter into covenant to serve God. On being told that he was, the priest said "then give your heart to God and your hand to me." Holding the child by the right hand, he then placed his left hand upon the youthful head, confirmed him as a member of the Lutheran church and exhorted him to faithfulness or indulged in predictions concerning his future, apparently as the spirit prompted him. Of one boy he expressed regret that he had been confirmed a Lutheran, for he would soon abandon the faith. The sequel proved this prediction to be true, for the boy soon left his birthplace to live among relatives who were Baptists, and accordingly became a Baptist.

When Niels was confirmed, the priest proceeded to say: "The Lord has laid a heavy hand upon you in your youth, which will be a hard cross for you to bear through life; but it was for a wise purpose—to prepare you for a great work that you do not understand now. After you have traveled thousands of miles to a strange land you know not, you will there eventually have a chance to go into the sanctuary of the Lord to do a work for your father's family and your ancestors that they did not understand or know anything about."

This prediction made a deep impression upon the mind of Niels, who remembered every word of it, and felt that somehow it would be fulfilled, though he could not then conceive how or when. That he, a helpless cripple and confirmed invalid; without money or influential friends, should ever travel thousands of miles over land and sea, seemed very improbable; indeed, it seemed very unlikely that he would live long enough to make such a journey if he were financially able.

CHAPTER II

DEATH OF HIS MOTHER—LIFE IN AALBORG—CONVERSION TO MORMONISM—HEAVENLY MESSAGE TO ELDER KEMPE—HIS OBEDIENCE THERETO—BAPTISM OF NIELS—HIS RELATIVES ASHAMED OF HIM—PROPOSITION TO MAKE HIM A LUTHERAN PREACHER.

If the details of the life of Niels for the next six years were written it would be a record of helpless dependence and privation. To the surprise of all who knew him, he continued to live, and even gain a little strength. Life at home had become unbearable since the death of his mother, which occurred December 6, 1854.

In the fall of 1856, when he was twenty years of age, Niels left home and went to live among relatives in Aalborg, where he had a checkered experience, often being made to feel that he was in the way and that his welcome was worn out, but occasionally encouraged by real kindness and genuine charity. One lady in particular took a great interest in him, and, finding that he had some skill in needle work, encouraged him to practice a kind that was much in vogue among ladies, and through her kindly efforts he obtained considerable profitable work from many aristocratic women.

Soon after removing to Aalborg he met and became somewhat acquainted with some "Mormons," a family of Saints being close neighbors to his aunt. His partial investigation of the Gospel then confirmed his early conviction that it was the truth, but his dependent condition, and the opposition of his relatives to such an unpopular religion, led him to defer embracing it.

It was not until November 1, 1862, six years after he first attended a "Mormon" meeting, that he embraced the Gospel, and then under peculiar circumstances. Christoffer Jensen Kempe, who afterwards became well known in Utah and Arizona, was laboring as a "Mormon" missionary in that part of Denmark. One very stormy night he had found lodgings in a barn, about forty-two miles from Aalborg. Some time after retiring to rest he was aroused by feeling a hand laid upon his shoulder and hearing a voice tell him to get up and go to Aalborg and baptize the cripple, Larsen, whom he had seen at the Saints' meetings—that if he ever joined the church he would have to be baptized the next evening. Obedient to the voice of the spirit, he arose and set out afoot in the storm. He walked the entire distance, and on his arrival in Aalborg he called upon Niels at his lodgings and informed him that he had come to baptize him. Niels immediately asked what prompted him to come, as he had not even announced his intention of joining the church. Elder Kempe related the visitation he had received forty-two miles distant, and told of his journey for the special purpose, and added that he would like while he was at it to baptize Niels' brother and sister-in-law who were then living in Aalborg, and whom he had met and talked with on the subject of religion. Niels ventured the opinion that neither of the relatives mentioned had any serious intention of embracing "Mormonism," and that he was sure they would not if they learned their crippled brother intended to do so. "However," he said, "you may try them, and if you succeed in getting their consent you may call back for me, and I will be ready."

The Elder promptly repaired to the brother's house and broached the subject of baptism to the couple, saying he was going to do some baptizing that night, and if they wished he would baptize them. They at first favored the proposition, but when he, hoping to hasten and make certain their decision, mentioned that Niels was going to be baptized they lost all interest in the subject and refused to be baptized.

Returning to Niels, the Elder informed him of his failure and disappointment. Niels was not at all surprised, and told the Elder he should not be disappointed in him, as he was ready. They accordingly made their way that very night a considerable distance out of town, to find a suitable place for the performance of the ordinance, and Niels was initiated into the Church by baptism November 1, 1862.

Some circumstances of which Niels was in ignorance at the time of his baptism, but which he afterwards learned of, may furnish the sequel to what was meant by the heavenly warning to Elder Kempe that Niels would have to be baptized that very evening if he ever joined the church at all.

Something like consternation had prevailed among the aristocratic members of the Lutheran church in and around Aalborg about that time, in consequence of so many of the members being converted to "Mormonism." As a rule they were not the wealthy members who accepted of the Gospel, as taught by the "Mormon" missionaries, but they included those who had been regarded as among the very best and most faithful members of the church, and they were joining the "Mormon" ranks in such numbers that they seemed for awhile to threaten the very existence of some of the Lutheran congregations.

The priests and their influential, loyal supporters held numerous meetings, to discuss measures for checking this defection and restoring the waning fealty of their flocks. Among other schemes resorted to was that of organizing a society or club among the wealthy women of the Church, and the collecting by them of a large sum of money, to effect a kind of revival in the church. The lady mentioned as having taken such an interest in procuring work for Niels was one of the leaders in this movement. She had discovered that Niels was a very observant individual, was a logical reasoner, had a most retentive memory and a very thorough knowledge of the scriptures. It had been her habit while Niels was employed at her home to test him upon these points. Occasionally she would ask him what the preacher had talked about at the service on the previous Sabbath, or to relate some particular thing that he had heard or read. He would not only be able to repeat, almost verbatim what he had heard or read, but to mimic the gestures of the speakers as well.

Possibly she and her aristocratic associates had been impressed with his mental vigor and been led to think that he might be utilized in some way in arousing an interest in church affairs. Possibly it may have been sympathy for him and the kindness of their hearts that prompted them to think of him in connection with their revival project. What they did was to get up a numerously signed petition to the bishop of the diocese, to appoint Niels to act as a lay preacher or exhorter—a kind of home missionary—to visit the members at their homes, hold semi-private services, etc., and to be paid a regular stipend therefor out of the funds they had collected. It could not have been anything attractive about his personality that suggested him for such a position, for in appearance he was repellant rather than attractive. Even the very dogs on the street shunned him or snarled at him and refused to be friendly or sociable with him. It could not have been any zeal that he manifested in the Lutheran church that caused him to be thought of, for although he frequently attended the Lutheran service (more as a matter of policy than otherwise, for he obtained his employment chiefly from the Lutheran ladies) he even more commonly attended the Latter-day Saint services, and had several times been chided by his Lutheran acquaintances for doing so. Of course Niels was not consulted in regard to the plans of the Lutheran ladies concerning him. His projected appointment was intended to be a surprise to him. The bishop announced to the ladies' society that he had complied with their petition and appointed Niels to act as lay preacher on the very day of the latter's baptism, as already mentioned, and that evening a meeting was held in the local Lutheran church, and the announcement was made public. The inquiry was then made of the congregation as to where Niels lived, so that the news might be sent to him, but no person present seemed to know. One man, however, arose in the congregation and volunteered the information that he was acquainted with the brother of Niels (the same one whom Elder Kempe had hoped to baptize,) and that he could carry the news to him of the honor that had come to Niels. He was accordingly commissioned to do so, but when he went to the brother the following day he learned to his surprise that he was just one day too late; Niels had embraced "Mormonism" the night before. He knew it, for he had witnessed the baptism.

Niels learned, soon after he was confirmed a Latter-day Saint, of the proposition to make him a preacher of the Lutheran religion, and of course was surprised thereat. He didn't regret having missed the opportunity. Being sure (as he had been ever since he was a child) that "Mormonism" was true, he would have had to stultify himself to advocate any other creed. He was glad, however, that the temptation never was squarely presented to him, lest in his weakness and poverty he might have yielded to it.

CHAPTER III

DESIRE TO MIGRATE—DISCOURAGING PROSPECTS—
HELP FROM AN UNEXPECTED SOURCE—RELIGIOUS
DISCRIMINATION—CONTENDS FOR HIS RIGHTS—
EFFECTS A COMPROMISE—CHARACTERISTICS OF
NIELS—SPIRITUAL IMPRESSIONS AND
PREMONITIONS.

In common with all the Saints in Scandinavia at that period, Niels had a strong desire to migrate to Zion, and was as ready as any of his countrymen to accomplish that end by rigid economy and self denial; but how he was ever going to obtain the price of his fare was a problem for which he could see no solution. His income from charity and his own earnings had been so meagre and precarious for years that it had been his habit from necessity to test how little it required to sustain life. To accumulate anything honestly had practically been out of the question. How then could he ever hope to save so large an amount as his fare to Utah would cost?

In the face of this discouraging prospect help came to him from a most unexpected source, which Niels has ever since regarded as providential. He had become acquainted with a kind hearted Lutheran priest, whose sympathy was doubtless excited by his helpless, dependent condition. One day when they chanced to meet, the priest mentioned the fact that a person had recently died who for several years previous had been enjoying a legacy bequeathed to the parish many years before by a charitable person, when about to die. One of the conditions of this bequest was that it should be held for the support of some worthy person who was physically helpless and dependent. Niels was reminded that he was physically and morally qualified to benefit by that legacy, and encouraged by the suggestion that he might possibly succeed as its beneficiary if he made application to the parish officers. He did so without delay, and to his great gratification he was granted the benefit of the legacy. It was not very much—it only amounted to about ten dollars per quarter, or $40.00 per year—but by maintaining the same system of economy he had previously practiced, he managed to save the greater part of it, and began to look forward to the time when his savings would be sufficient to pay for his emigration.

Niels had not enjoyed this legacy very long, however, when the parish officers learned that he was a "Mormon," and stopped payment of the stipend. They soon found, though, that Niels was not to be disposed of so easily. Friendless and helpless and cripple though he was, he was not lacking in courage and a sense of the justice of his cause. Boldly he went before the parish officers and demanded the payment of the stipend that had been withheld, and its continuance while he lived. Assuming that the person who made the bequest had not stipulated that it should be held exclusively for Lutherans, he charged that they had no right to apply any religious test to him, and defended his cause so well that his hearers were forced to admit that he was right. After a very lengthly parley they reluctantly offered to compromise by allowing him the benefit of the legacy for a limited time. He refused the offer and contended for his life interest, and reminded them that notwithstanding his weakly condition he was liable to live a long time, as his ancestors had been noted for their longevity. When they were thoroughly impressed with this possibility, he offered a compromise—proposing that the amount of twelve quarterly payments be advanced to him from the funds of the legacy, on condition that he surrender his right to any more, and migrate to Utah. This they finally agreed to, and thus Niels was enabled to come to Utah with a company of Saints which left Copenhagen May 17, 1866.

Before mentioning the details of the journey or his life in Utah it may be appropriate to revert to some things that tend to illustrate the character of Niels. He is possessed of a strong and independent mind, fixed convictions and marvelous will power for one whose body is so frail. His spirituality is highly developed; but one would not know it from his manner. He is never exuberant, enthusiastic or talkative, but sedate, reserved and self-possessed. He is a keen observer, a good listener, a logical and discriminating thinker and a thoughtful and discreet talker. He has a high sense of honor, a respect for others' rights and feelings, charity for the weaknesses and failings of others, and for one who has been so helplessly dependent the greater part of his life, is wonderfully free from servility. He is grateful for kindness and favors shown him, but never truculent or even obsequious. He has reasons satisfactory to himself for his actions, but these reasons are not always apparent to others, and because of this his motives have often been misconstrued, even by his friends and co-religionists. He has few confidants, and lives as it were in a world of his own, being reticent to a marked degree, but confident and self-reliant as to his course in life. Though diffident about admitting it, his spiritual impressions have largely controlled his actions throughout his life. When only ten years old the premonition of impending disaster was so strong within him, that just prior to the dreadful accident which left him maimed for life, he plead with his parents not to send him for the cow, and when they persisted in doing so, warned them that they would be sorry for if all their lives. They did not mean to be unkind or heartless; indeed, they had great love for their children, and the father was especially indulgent; but they had strict ideas in regard to family discipline, and when once the word of either one was passed as to any requirement on the part of the children, both were unyielding in demanding compliance. They saw no danger in his bringing the cow in from the pasture. He had done so many times before, without any harm resulting therefrom, and they saw no reason why he should not do so again, with impunity. The sequel, however, proved that his premonition was correct.

CHAPTER IV

A VISION AND ITS PRE-MORTAL COUNTERPART—
BESET BY EVIL SPIRITS—DELIVERANCE THEREFROM—
PREPARATIONS TO MIGRATE—LONG VOYAGE—
TOILSOME JOURNEY—LOST ON THE PLAINS—HELP
FROM THE LORD.

His crippled, helpless condition was a great source of sorrow to Niels, and instead of his becoming gradually reconciled thereto, as it might be supposed that he would, he seemed to brood over it more the older he grew. He belonged to a proud and rather dignified family, and was naturally very proud himself, but realized that he did not present a dignified appearance. He was constantly reminded that people were repelled rather than attracted by him, and this of course wounded his pride and made him miserable.

During the summer preceding his baptism, after a day of extreme melancholy, an incident occurred that produced an entire change in his feelings. While engaged preparing his evening meal a glorious vision burst upon his view. It was not a single scene that he beheld, but a series of them. He compares them to the modern moving pictures, for want of a better illustration. He beheld as with his natural sight, but he realized afterwards that it was with the eye of the spirit that he saw what he did. His understanding was appealed to as well as his sight. What was shown him related to his existence in the spirit world, mortal experience and future rewards. He comprehended, as if by intuition, that he had witnessed a somewhat similar scene in his pre-mortal state, and been given the opportunity of choosing the class of reward he would like to attain to. He knew that he had deliberately made his choice. He realized which of the rewards he had selected, and understood that such a reward was only to be gained by mortal suffering—that, in fact, he must be a cripple and endure severe physical pain, privation and ignominy. He was conscious too that he still insisted upon having that reward, and accepted and agreed to the conditions.

He emerged from the vision with a settled conviction that to rebel against or even to repine at his fate, was not only a reproach to an Alwise Father whose care had been over him notwithstanding his seeming abandonment, but a base violation of the deliberate promise and agreement he had entered into, and upon the observance of which his future reward depended.

Whatever opinion others may entertain concerning the philosophy involved in this theory, is a matter of absolute indifference to Niels. He does not advocate it; he does not seek to apply it to any other case; but he has unshaken faith in it so far as his own case is concerned. Whether true or not, the fact remains that he has derived comfort, satisfaction, resolution and fortitude from it. He has ever since been resigned to his affliction, and, though never mirthful, is serene and composed and uncomplaining. He has always felt that the vision was granted to him by the Lord for a wise and merciful purpose—that he might, through a better understanding of his duty, be able to remain steadfast thereto.

In striking contrast to this experience was that which occurred during the night following his baptism. Evil spirits seemed to fill the room in which he had retired to sleep. They were not only terribly visible, but he heard voices also, taunting him with having acted foolishly in submitting to baptism and joining the Latter-day Saints. He was told that he had deserted the only friends he ever had, and would find no more among the "Mormons," who would allow him to die of starvation rather than assist him. That he had no means of earning a livlihood in the far western land to which the Saints all hoped to migrate, and he would never cease to regret it if he ever went there. This torment was kept up incessantly until he sought relief in prayer, and three times he got out of bed and tried to pray before he succeeded in doing so. Then his fervent pleading unto the Lord for power to withstand the temptation of the evil one, and to hold fast to the truth, brought relief to him. The evil spirits gradually, and with apparent reluctance, withdrew, and peace came to his soul, with the assurance that the Lord approved of his embracing the Gospel, and that he could safely rely upon the Lord for future guidance.

Preparations were soon made to migrate to Utah, although Niels was seriously ill. In addition to his other troubles, he had for years been afflicted with asthma, and he had such difficulty in breathing that for a long time he had not been able to recline, having to sleep, if at all, in a sitting posture. He was also so frail and weak at the time that many of his acquaintances expressed a fear that he would not live to make the journey, and some even predicted that he would die while crossing the ocean. Not at all daunted, however, by these pessimists, he determined to start with the very first company of migrating Saints, and soon arranged with a newly-married couple and a young single man who were ambitious to migrate, to care for him on the journey, carry and look after his luggage, etc., in return for certain financial aid which he was able and willing to afford them. He realized that it would be a long and tiresome trip, and his natural independence was exhibited in thus arranging beforehand for the help he might require, lest he might be regarded as a public burden. The journey, as planned, was not as direct as those commonly pursued in more recent years, nor nearly so expeditious. The company assembled at Copenhagen, whence they proceeded by steamer to Kiel, in Germany, and from there took train for Altonia. At Hamburg, on the river Elbe, they boarded an ocean sailing vessel, the "Kenilworth," bound for New York. The voyage lasted eight weeks, long enough for the passengers to get well acquainted with one another.

They had expected to proceed westward from New York, (or rather from the New Jersey side of the Hudson river) by rail, but Thomas Taylor, who was the Church Immigration Agent in New York at that time, had learned before their arrival that all the lines of railway extending westward from that point had entered into a combine to demand a higher rate for transporting companies of Latter-day Saints than those previously prevailing. Determined not to submit to their extortion, he discovered before the company arrived that one line of railway extending westward from New Haven, Connecticut, was not in the combine, and would transport the company at the old rate, and he decided to patronize it. The road was either poorly equipped with cars or lacked time before the arrival of the company to make the necessary arrangements for convenient transportation.

The accommodations on the train as it was made up were rather meager; in fact, it was a cattle car that Niels rode in, and the passengers had to sit or he on the floor. The road bed appeared to lack ballast, and the ride was a jolty, tiresome one—particularly hard on Niels, who was so painfully affected by the jolting that he sought relief by bracing his hands against the floor on either side of him, thereby partially sustaining the weight of his body and easing the jar. The shaking was so great that both doors fell off the car, and, to cap the climax, some of the cars ran off the track, the one in which Niels rode standing crosswise of the track, and with two of the wheels broken off it, when the train came to a halt. This occurred on the bank of a river in Southern Canada, and the passengers breathed a sigh of relief when they discovered what a narrow escape they had from being plunged into the river.

From New York the company therefore proceeded by coast steamer to New Haven, and from there by train to St. Joseph Missouri, where they were transferred to a river boat that during the next two days took them up the Missouri to Wyoming Hills, a few miles from Nebraska City, from which point they were to be conveyed by ox train to Salt Lake City, more than a thousand miles distant.

Before leaving Denmark, he had not been able to walk as much as two hundred yards without stopping to rest, but he gradually improved while crossing the sea, and, though temporarily prostrated with the heat while on the river steamer, he rallied before the overland journey was undertaken. Before starting from the Missouri river the able-bodied passengers were requested to walk as much as possible on the journey, as the wagons were heavily loaded and the strength of the oxen had to be conserved, as they had an eight weeks trip before them.

Though far from being able-bodied, Niels determined to do his best at walking. He accordingly set out bravely with the other pedestrians, with whom, however, he was unable to keep up, as his gait was like that of a snail. His habit was to walk until overtaken by the train, or until he was so fatigued that he could not proceed further, when he would get into a wagon and ride. Occasionally he succeeded by perseverance in walking all day long, and was necessarily most of the time alone. By starting early, as soon as breakfast was over, and before the teams had been hitched up, he would be able to keep ahead of the train, and yet soon be outdistanced by his more able companions. Upon one occasion he got lost as a result of being alone. He arrived at a point where the road which he was following diverged into two. Not knowing which of the two he should take, he happened to choose the wrong one, and traveled for a long distance without being able to see those who had preceded him or the wagons in the rear. Without apprehension, he trudged along until he arrived at a river which was too deep and swift for him to wade, and which was spanned by a rude foot bridge, consisting of two or three lengths of a single round pole, supported where the ends joined amid-stream by two poles set up in the form of a cross, with the lower ends firmly imbedded in the stream, and securely lashed with rawhide at the intersection. The swiftness of the current and the distance from the foot bridge down to the stream made him dizzy when he looked down, so that he despaired of being able to cross the bridge, and yet felt that he must do so to overtake the train that he supposed must have forded at a point much lower down stream. In his emergency he knelt in prayer on the river bank, reminding the Lord of his dependence upon Him and appealing unto Him for help. He arose with a feeling of confidence, and without any trepidation or dizziness set out and walked along the pole as steadily as if he had been a tight-rope performer. Then, following his impression as to the course he ought to take, he walked on until he overtook the train, encamped, some time after nightfall, and when men were about to be dispatched to search for him.

CHAPTER V

FEAT AS A PEDESTRIAN—LESSONS LEARNED AND AMBITION DEVELOPED WHILE TRAVELING—ARRIVAL IN SALT LAKE CITY—EMPLOYMENT DILIGENTLY SOUGHT—PRECARIOUS SUCCESS—MIRACULOUSLY FED.

The journey on the whole, though tiresome, was not otherwise unpleasant. He enjoyed the society of his fellow emigrants, and felt that he had been blessed of the Lord beyond his most sanguine hopes; for notwithstanding his feeble condition when starting, he succeeded in walking more than three fourths of the way across the plains. He had also been cured of the asthma with which he had been so long afflicted—not suddenly, but so gradually that he hardly realized that he was outgrowing it.

He had also been benefited otherwise by the experience gained on the journey. His views of life had become broadened by travel, and by the evidences of thrift and enterprise which he witnessed on his journey through the states, as well as by the possibilities of development he could forsee in the great and boundless west. He felt like a bird released from a cage after a lengthy confinement therein. He enjoyed his freedom and learned to commune with Nature as he never had done before. His knowledge of human nature had also been very materially added to since leaving his native land. There are few conditions under which human nature can be studied to better advantage than while making such a journey over sea and land as that which he had passed through. The crowding together of a large company in the hold of a ship for eight long weeks, with meagre accommodations and food generally insufficient and frequently bad, is certain to develop selfishness, impatience and irritability where these qualities exist even in latent form. His fellow passengers were actuated by the noblest motives in migrating. They had accepted the Gospel of the Lord Jesus Christ, some of them at the sacrifice of material comforts, and most of them at the cost of friends and prestige. Some of them had been sneered at and persecuted in their native land, and had their former friends and relatives turn to be their bitter enemies, solely because of their accepting of and adhering to such an unpopular creed. They had withstood all that, and, with faith still unshaken, were willing to brave other trials and face the hardships of this long voyage and journey, and the problems incident to life in a new and wild country, to gain religious freedom, and because they regarded it as a divine requirement. But human nature, even though tempered by religious convictions, is apt to assert itself sometimes, and the helpless, dependent condition of Niels placed him in the position of a spectator, with ample opportunity to observe all that passed, and to study human nature during the voyage as he never had done before.

Disputes occasionally arose among the passengers, which sometimes waxed warm and developed into angry quarrels, all of which Niels noticed but never took part in. Possibly because he was always an observer of but never a participant in these affairs, he was several times appealed to as an arbitrator, to decide between the disputants and effect a reconciliation. Without making any pretentions to judicial wisdom, he was, through strict impartiality, and tact in offering reproof without giving offense, and especially by appealing to the religious obligations of the parties to the strife, enabled to do effective work as a peace-maker, and to gain respect therefor. He couldn't refrain from indulging in a little mental philosophy on such occasions, and making note of the fact that the tongue is a dangerous member if allowed to wag too freely.

Three times during the voyage the ship had taken fire, always at night, as a result of the cook's carelessness, and a general panic among the passengers, if nothing worse, was narrowly averted. Upon the first of these occasions the fire had gained sufficient headway before it was discovered for a rather large bole to be burned through the floor almost directly above where Niels had his bunk, and when the first alarm was sounded Niels looked upward and saw the fire and noticed the presence of smoke in the hold. He was able to "keep his head" and helped in some measure in quelling the excitement of his fellows, many of whom became almost frantic when they learned that the ship was on fire, and that the hatches were fastened down, so that the passengers were shut up in the hold like rats in a trap.

It occurred to Niels that the hatches had been closed by order of the ship's officers to prevent a panic. He saw the futility of rebelling against the measure, and counseled calmness and patience; and was so calm and self-possessed himself that some of the more excited ones listened to him, made a strong effort to control themselves, and seemed ashamed at having been overcome by alarm.

The overland journey on the cars and the eight weeks' trip by ox train in crossing the plains were not less fruitful in opportunities to study character under trying conditions, and for the personal display of those amenities that distinguish gentility from boorishness and Christian charity from heartless selfishness. It was alike creditable to the restraining influence of the Gospel upon the company in general, and to the fine discernment and keen discrimination of Niels, that he did not lose faith in his fellows because of the weakness they exhibited under trying conditions— that he arrived in Utah with a keener appreciation of the Gospel's power to mold human character to conform to the divine pattern. He too had been tried as never before in his life, and the consciousness of his own failings made him charitable for those of others.

Some of his experiences on the plains had a peculiarly western flavor. Although the company of which he was a member never actually came in conflict with the Indians, they had a number of thrills due to rumors of Indian hostilities before or behind them. One night the ox train emigrant company camped on one side of a river which they expected to cross early the next morning, while a mule train loaded with merchandise camped on the opposite bank of the same stream. During the night a marauding band of Indians stole and ran off about ninety head of mules from the train last mentioned, driving them all right past the camp of the passenger train, and so close to it that Niels heard them galloping by, and wondered at first whether the noise was caused by the oxen stampeding. Another experience that was new and strange to him was seeing a rattle snake dart into a hole over which he was about to make his bed. It didn't produce a very comfortable feeling, but the bed was made right over the hole and the snake created no disturbance during the night.

Before the journey ended Niels began to feel almost as if he were a western man himself, so thoroughly had he entered into the spirit of all that pertained to it. He had engaged in a struggle with a large number of fellows for a common goal, and had developed ability that he had never before known himself to be possessed of, and now, on reaching it, he was ambitious to be a factor in the further unfolding of God's purposes.

On his arrival in Salt Lake City Niels sought employment by which to earn a subsistence, for he could not bear the thought of being always dependent upon others. He found, however, that such work as he was capable of doing was neither remunerative nor easily obtained. His first job was at glove-making. He found two of his fellow country women engaged in the business of making and selling buckskin gloves, their customers in the main being overland travelers. He persuaded them to let him learn the business from them, and then furnish him employment when they had more work than they could do themselves. The work was precarious at best, and not at all lucrative, but he appreciated having anything to do, and being able to earn ever so little. After attaining to some skill in that line, the demand for buckskin gloves fell off until there was no longer any encouragement to make them. Then he learned to sew uppers for ladies' shoes, and obtained a limited amount of work in that line, but machines soon displaced hand sewing of shoes. His means of earning a livelihood seemed to be diminishing rather than increasing, but with independence unabated, he sought work at whatever he could do (which was almost exclusively limited to sewing) and went without what he could not earn, or which did not come to him voluntarily, without making his wants known. In a land of plenty, surrounded by people who were amply able to help him, and who would willingly have shared with him their last meal, he lived almost like a recluse, and sometimes actually suffered for want of food. Two or three instances of uncharitableness and lack of sympathy sealed his lips against any admission of his real condition or complaint, and nerved him up to go without what he could not earn, or die trying. How little he subsisted upon for certain extended periods is almost beyond belief, and he probably would not have lived to tell it had not the Lord mercifully and miraculously replenished his larder as He did in the case of the widow of old who fed the prophet Elijah. Many times he scraped up the last saucerful of flour to make a cake, only to find as much more in the sack when hunger again impelled him to search for it. And so it happened that while his faith in mankind sometimes wavered, his faith in the Almighty grew stronger.

It must not be supposed from this that he was wholly without friends, or that his existence was a cheerless one; but he had an aversion to testing the friendship of his fellows by making known his wants, and a feeling that his friends would last longer if not used too much. He had entirely too much independence for a pauper, and too little bodily strength to competently make his way in the world without help. His circumstances varied. Sometimes for a considerable period fortune would favor him to a limited extent, his health being such that he could search for and obtain work and accumulate a little. He had the thrifty disposition that characterized the Scandinavian race, and his natural bent was to save some portion of it, however little he might earn. He had the "home-making" instinct as it would be termed if he were a bird—the disposition to build or acquire a nest of his own, however humble it might be, and so he labored to that end. In this, however, he met with many reverses. Illness would occasionally befall him, and his petty hoard would be exhausted before he could again resume his earning and saving. At quite an early stage of his Utah existence he invested five dollars, the savings of a long period, in a city lot in what is now the Twenty-seventh Ward of Salt Lake City, at a time when lots on the north bench, away above the inhabited district, could be had for the price of surveying. He could not afford to build upon it; in fact, it was only by heroic effort that he succeeded in paying the small tax upon it from year to year; but at the inception of the boom in real estate in 1888 he succeeded in selling that lot for $500.00. The possibility of owning a home loomed up before him as it never had done before, and from that time he began looking for a bargain in real estate.

CHAPTER VI

INVESTS IN REAL ESTATE—ACQUIRES A HOME—
VICARIOUS WORK IN LOGAN TEMPLE—CONSEQUENT
ELATION—PROMISE TO A DYING FRIEND—
GRATUITOUS FULFILLMENT IN MANTI TEMPLE.

In the course of a few years he found an opportunity of buying a small city lot north west of the capital grounds, with a rather old house upon it, for the modest sum which his capital represented, and he actually became a landlord. He rented part of it to the former owner, who had lost the property through mortgaging it and being unable to meet the payments when his notes fell due. His income from the rental was only $5.00 per month, and it required half of that to pay the taxes upon the property; but he had a shelter for himself as well—not very comfortable it was true, but much more so than some of the houses he had occupied—and it was his own. It was all the more appreciated when he thought of the improbability of his ever owning a home of any kind had he remained in his native land. He could now look forward with more hope to his declining years, when age would naturally add to his decrepitude.

When Niels accepted of the Gospel in his native land, no feature of it was more attractive to him than the promise of salvation for the dead contained therein. He found comfort in the assurance he obtained of personal salvation through compliance with the Gospel principles, and he was anxious to do something if possible that his ancestors and friends who had died without a knowledge of the Gospel should share in the Gospel privileges. When the Temple in Logan was completed and opened for ordinance work, he joyfully journeyed thither and spent eight weeks in receiving ordinances for the benefit of dead relatives. He felt that he was coming into his own, that he was accomplishing something that made life desirable. There was something exalting about the thought that he, deformed and weak and frail though he was, could do all for the salvation of his dead kindred and friends that the most able-bodied man in the community could do. He had long admired the missionaries who left their homes in Utah and the surrounding states, and, at infinite sacrifice, went forth into the

various nations of the earth to proclaim the Gospel message, without hope of earthly reward. The sole reason for their doing so was that they had been called by those whom they regarded as the Lord's earthly representatives to so labor, and because they regarded the Gospel as so priceless that they were anxious to have its benefits extended to all humanity. He, too, appreciated the Gospel, and his love for his fellows would have enabled him to find joy in laboring as a missionary, but, alas! he could never hope to engage in that labor because of his physical disabilities. But here was a labor which had for its object the same purpose, in which in point of ability he measured up to the full stature of the best of his fellows; and who should say that the work done in behalf of the dead is not just as important as that done for the living? He had never engaged in anything that so increased his self respect and made him feel that he was of some consequence in the world as this work in the Temple, and he regretted when necessity compelled him to abandon this labor which had such a savor of heaven about it and "come down to earth," figuratively speaking, by seeking such employment as he could engage in to earn the meagre necessaries of his subsistence.

A considerable period passed afterward with little to relieve the monotony of his existence, during which, however, he again succeeded in accumulating something. In the meantime the Temple at Manti had been completed and ordinance work was being performed therein.

It happened that an old gentleman named Nielsen with whom Niels had years before, (while he was a resident of Salt Lake City,) been somewhat acquainted, had located at Manti while the Temple was in course of construction, and indulged in the hope of spending his declining years in laboring therein for the benefit of his dead kindred. Before being able or ready so to do, however, he had been stricken with sickness, and, at the solicitation of a daughter who was living in Salt Lake City, and who was the wife of a Catholic, had come up to reside with her and be nursed back to health. Instead of recovering, however, he continued to grow worse until his life was despaired of. During his illness he worried constantly over the fact that the work in the Temple which his heart had been so set upon performing for his dead kindred had never been done, and there now seemed no hope of his doing it, for he felt that he must soon die. In his emergency he thought about Niels as a friend whose services he might enlist, and induced his daughter to send for him to come and listen to her father's dying request. Niels came, and found his old friend almost in the throes of death. Being asked if he would do the work in the Temple which his friend had neglected, he consented without hesitancy, to pacify the dying man, and wrote down at his dictation the names of about seventy of his dead relatives, in whose behalf he wished the work performed. He was told that a certain sister living in Manti had promised to perform the work for the females, and could be relied upon to do so, and that it would only be necessary for him to see that she did it, and to do himself the work for the males.

After receiving the promise from Niels that he would attend to the matter, the old gentleman seemed satisfied, and soon died in peace. Niels then realized, as he had not done before, the responsibility that rested upon him, in consequence of his promise. He had never made a promise even to a person who was well without faithfully fulfilling it, and his promise made to a dying man seemed doubly binding. He must fulfill that if he never lived to do anything else. With this impressed upon his mind he soon journeyed to Manti and called upon the sister who had promised his dead friend to serve in the Temple for the female relatives. He found her so ill that there was little hope of her ever being able to keep her promise, and so he conscientiously applied himself to the task of fulfilling completely the commission assigned him. He hired sisters to do the work for the female dead, and he spent ten weeks in the Manti Temple, in constant labor for the male dead kindred of his friend Nielsen, and felt satisfaction in having done all that duty and honor could require of him in the matter.

CHAPTER VII

COMPLETION OF SALT LAKE TEMPLE—HIS WORK THEREIN—SISTER CORRADI INSPIRED TO APPLY TO HIM—DEVOTED WORK FOR HER KINDRED—HIS SEVERE AFFLICTIONS—SAVING WORK FOR 2200—GRACEFUL OLD AGE.

Niels looked forward with fond anticipation to the completion of the Salt Lake Temple. He felt that now, that he had found his true vocation, he would like to devote all the time to Temple work that his health and means would permit, and he could do this to much better advantage in his home city than if he had to travel a long distance to reach a Temple, and then make special arrangements for his board and lodging. He commenced his labors three weeks after the Temple opened for ordinance work. He not only found great comfort and satisfaction in the work, (which he scrupulously devoted his time to whenever able to do so,) but, through the acquaintances he formed there, he obtained a considerable amount of employment in the sewing line, especially in the making of temple clothing, at which he became quite an expert. He was not able to work continuously; indeed, he had many spells of illness that confined him to the house and occasionally to his bed for days and weeks at a time, but he has long been known as one of the most earnest and devoted workers in the Temple. When he had officiated for all his dead kindred and friends concerning whom he had sufficiently definite information, he found others who were anxious to have him officiate for their dead kindred on the usual terms when men are so employed, (seventy-five cents per day,) and he so labored whenever able to do so. He has, however, officiated gratuitously for hundreds of people at the instance of friends or relatives who were unable to pay therefor. A case in point was that of a poor Scandinavian sister who died a few years since in this city. She left a list of fifty dead relatives for whom she had been unable to officiate, and he took up the work for the males and hunted up women acquaintances who were willing to officiate for the females.

A few years since he was called upon by a Sister Corradi, whom he only knew by sight, who desired to employ him to officiate for her male kindred dead, saying the Spirit had manifested to her that he was the person to whom she should apply. He consented, and has worked almost exclusively for her list since, and has enough names left to keep him occupied for about another year. Having a spell of illness some time since, he told Sister Corradi she had better find some one else to finish her work, as he feared he might not be able to do so. She, however, refused to believe that he was going to die soon, or fail to finish her work, and said she knew he was going to live to do it. She may be right. Now that he has lived so long (he was seventy-eight years old in May) there is reason to hope that he has several years yet to remain in mortality. It will soon be forty-eight years since he arrived in Utah, notwithstanding the predictions that he would not live to make the journey. It is nearly sixty-eight years since he met with the accident that left him deformed and crippled for life, and during that time he has never been free from pain, though it has varied in degree, being much more intense at some times than others. For many years hernia was added to his other afflictions, but he was healed of that in answer to prayer. About four years ago he lost the use of his voice, and has not since been able to speak above a whisper. In spite, however, of all these handicaps he has accomplished a work of self-sacrifice for the salvation of others that any able-bodied man of his age, desiring the welfare of his fellows, might well be proud of. He has officiated for fully twenty-two hundred persons in all the temple ordinances necessary to place them on a par with the living who have received these ordinances in their own behalf. All this in addition to the work he has had done in behalf of numerous female dead. Truly he has earned for himself the distinction of being a "Savior upon Mount Zion." The crucible of suffering to which he has been so long subjected has had a sanctifying and exalting effect upon him, and eliminated from his character all semblance of sordidness. His struggle for existence has developed the strong traits of his character that otherwise might have remained dormant, and his beneficent concern for others has helped him to bear with equanimity, if not to forget his own troubles. Even age seems to sit lightly upon him. Few who see him ever suspect his advanced age. The peevish, crabbed disposition that so frequently characterizes old age is never manifested by him. Instead, he wears the patient, serene expression of one who lives for a noble purpose, and indulges only in clean and wholesome thoughts.

CHAPTER VIII

A MODERN STOIC—HIS MODEST OBSCURITY—WHAT
RELIGION HAS DONE FOR NIELS—PHILOSOPHIC WAY
IN WHICH HE VIEWS DEATH.

Of the many who have witnessed Niels pursuing his toilsome way
between his home and the Temple—a distance of about a mile—
leaning upon his crutch and moving along at a slow but steady gait,
perhaps not one has had a definite idea of what a heroic effort it has
required for him to walk at all, and how his constant pain has been
increased thereby.

Perhaps none of his fellow workers in the temple, who are in the
daily habit of gazing upon his sphinx-like countenance as he silently
passes among them, ever even dream that he is the best modern
example of the stoic that this region has ever known, the physical
agony that he suffers being never betrayed by word or facial
expression.

Though casually known to many, he has scarcely been intimate with
any. Even the facts pertaining to his life that are herein divulged,
had to be fairly pried out of him by degrees, and they will doubtless
be a revelation to many of his acquaintances when they read this
recital. If his real condition had been generally known in the past,
his every want would have been anticipated and supplied by his
kind-hearted neighbors or the relief society. The chivalrous boy
scouts might have adopted him as their protege, and done what they
could to make his home cheerful, or otherwise lighten his burdens,
and dyspeptics and other victims of luxurious living might have
been making pilgrimages to his house to learn the secret of his long
and useful life under such unfavorable conditions.

Possibly it is as well that he has been allowed to make his own way
in the world. If he had been petted and pampered, and not had the
incentive of want to spur him to exertion, he probably would never

have accomplished anything worth mentioning, or that would have distinguished him from the great number of unfortunates that only excite our pity.

Niels acknowledges his indebtedness to the Gospel for all the comfort he has experienced in life. Indeed, without its sustaining power, it is doubtful whether he could have lived as long as he has, or retained his reason, if he had so lived. Without it, he could have had no desire to live; and, failing to find relief in death, his bodily suffering would probably have made of him a raving maniac or a driveling imbecile. As already mentioned, he was converted to the Gospel some time before he was baptized. He has never since entertained a doubt as to its truth. One might as well try to convince him that the sun does not shine, as that the Gospel is not true. Since his baptism he has been unwavering in his devotion to his religion. He has doubtless got more out of his religion than most adherents do. It has been the controlling inspiration of his life. He has been zealous, without being fanatical; devout, without outward expression. He has been a regular attendant at meetings (until he became in recent years too deaf to hear the preaching,) but never ambitious to take part therein. He feels amply repaid in the joy and satisfaction that have come to him for all the labors he has performed, and all the sufferings he has endured. He has no fear of death, but does not court it. He is content to live as long as the Lord is willing to have him do so [1]. He seeks no notoriety. He is the very

---

[1] 1. Niels has a very confident feeling that he will live to be 82 years of age, but whether the call comes to quit this mortal life sooner or later he intends to be prepared for it, and the completeness of his arrangements for his burial and for perpetuating a knowledge of his burial place indicates the complacency with which he regards death. Some time since he purchased a quarter of a lot in the cemetery, and had a very substantial granite monument made to his order and erected thereon. An inscription upon it gives his name, date and place of his birth, his parentage, and Salt Lake City as the place of his death, with blank space below upon which to chisel in the date of his passing away. He also keeps his burial clothes, made by himself, all nicely laundried, in readiness to place upon his body when death shall overtake him. This too is another illustration of his independence, and disposition to do things himself rather than trust to others.

personification of modesty. He is willing to be regarded as a grain of dust, an insignificant atom, and plod on in obscurity during the remainder of his mortal existence, as he has done in the past, without attracting any attention.

The author of this sketch has known Niels casually for years, but never discovered his real character until quite recently. For aught he knows, he may be the original discoverer. He regards as a very great compliment from Niels, the statement that he understood his character and motives as no one else had done before. He sought the acquaintance and confidence of Niels—was not sought by him. He it was, and not Niels, who conceived the idea of reducing to writing some of the incidents of his eventful life, and who surprised him later with a proposition to publish the same. The author is responsible for all deductions expressed herein, the facts alone having been somewhat reluctantly mentioned by Niels, but he has perused the story and endorsed it as correct, with some evident misgiving as to the possible resultant notoriety.

If benefits to the many constitute the true standard by which

---

Since the erection of his tombstone, a lady who was somewhat acquainted with him happened to be in the cemetery and saw it. She read the inscription with surprise and sorrow. She failed to notice that the date of his death was lacking, and very naturally concluded that he had died and been buried, and was surprised that it could have happened without the news of it having reached her. She mourned to think she would never see him again, and that she had not even attended his funeral and manifested the respect she had for one whose suffering and inoffensiveness had so strongly appealed to her. In a pensive mood she returned home and told her friends how shocked and sorrow stricken she was at learning for the first time on seeing his monument of the death of her friend.

A few days later she was tripping across Main Street without any thought of death in her mind, when she suddenly beheld his familiar figure slowly moving down the side walk. She was so startled at sight of what she thought must be an apparition that she stood transfixed until she was aroused by the hoot of an approaching automobile, and narrowly escaped being knocked down and run over.

success should be gauged, the life of Niels has certainly been a successful one; and the record herein set forth of the adverse conditions which have surrounded him, and his wonderful accomplishments in view thereof, should be an inspiration to every person who feels that his life's burden is heavy, and who is privileged to read this simple recital.

If the unselfish work to which Niels has devoted such a large part of his life had no other beneficial effect than to sweeten the lives and render lovable the characters of those who engage therein; to develop in them genuine love for their fellows and true charity—a willingness to benefit others without hope of reward therefor—and to make them cheerful, and hopeful and buoyant when otherwise they might be despondent and gloomy, surely that work is not in vain. Indeed it would even then compare favorably with almost any other that claims the attention of mankind.

If the "Mormon" theory be correct, the Gospel ordinances absolutely essential to the salvation and exaltation of mankind may be received by the living vicariously for the benefit of the dead. The dead, too, through an intelligent acceptance in the spirit world of the conditions of salvation, including the vicarious work voluntarily undertaken in their behalf on earth, may enjoy all the Gospel privileges.

Assuming that this theory is correct, what more important labor could a person engage in than that performed in the Temples? Is there any work on earth more free from the taint of selfishness? Is there anything a person could engage in that savors more of true Christian charity? Is not the satisfaction experienced by such earnest, sincere, conscientious people as Niels a strong evidence of the truth and efficacy of the work? Is not the assurance that Niels and thousands of others have received through the testimony of the Spirit, as to the work being acceptable to the dead in whose behalf it is done, and agreeable to the will of the Almighty, worthy of consideration?

The work done in the temple in behalf of the dead differs in this respect from other forms of charity—there is no danger of it making the one who performs it vainglorious. He is not open to the suspicion that the Pharisees of old were, in their giving of alms—a desire for applause, or "to be seen of men." Niels has not become puffed up because of what he has accomplished. He does not pose as anybody's benefactor. He assumes no heroic airs. There is no halo surrounding him such as "limners give to be the beloved disciple." He is just a modest, humble, obscure cripple, known to his neighbors, who are sufficiently acquainted with him to call him by name as Niels Larsen [2] ; who is content to live and die without attaining to any distinction, who is advertised for the first time in this recital, and this without any desire or request on his part. He

---

[2] A custom prevails very generally among the peasantry throughout Scandinavia of changing the surname from generation to generation, while among the aristocracy the rule is to maintain the same surname in a family as one generation succeeds another. An exception to this latter rule sometimes occurs when a branch of an aristocratic family does not inherit wealth, or through some misfortune becomes financially reduced, and has to take rank per force with the peasantry. Then, notwithstanding the aristocratic lineage, the peasant method of changing the surname of the progeny from father to son is followed.

As already mentioned in this narrative, Niels was of aristocratic lineage on both his father's and mother's side. They were, however, of minor branches that did not inherit much wealth. The father, though given in infancy the family surname of Eskildz, was known more generally throughout his lifetime by his given name of Lars Nielsen, and called Eskildz more as a nickname than otherwise, or as a means of distinguishing him from others having the name of Lars Nielsen. When Niels was born he was named Niels Larsen, in accordance with the peasant custom, and it was not until he commenced his work in the house of the Lord that he assumed his rightful ancestral name, and is even now scarcely known outside of the Temple by the name of Eskildz.

Niels' father and mother were second cousins. His mother's maiden name was Marie Olesen Myre. As may be inferred from the relationship existing between them before marriage, theirs was not the first marriage between the Eskildz and Myre families. Some branches of these two families were very wealthy and influential when Niels was a boy, which fact, however, was of no advantage to their poorer relatives, among whom were Niels and his parents.

was the most insignificant and unpromising (not to say despised) of all his kindred, the tag end, as it were, of the aristocratic and once powerful families from which he had descended. He is the only one of a numerous kindred (so far as known) who has accepted of the Gospel. Possibly others of them, as well as the brother and sister-in-law already mentioned, have rejected the Gospel because of their shame of him.

Is it not possible that this stone which these builders of the family's reputation rejected may yet become the chief corner? That this despised of all his race may yet become the head of it? In view of the vast work that he has accomplished in behalf of his progenitors, may we not anticipate the grateful homage that he will receive from them in the next world, when he, as a resurrected being, will stand in their midst—not as a cripple, deformed, and dwarfed, and weak, and racked with pain, as he has been during most of his mortal career, but resplendent in all the glory of a perfected manhood, his physical body conforming in stature and appearance to his spiritual body, a very king among his fellows! Imagine, too, the joyful acclaim with which he will then be greeted by the numerous host who are not of his immediate kindred, for whose salvation he has unselfishly labored in mortality. Then will the pain and suffering and fatigue and humiliation which he endured in this life seem as nothing compared with the treasures in heaven which he will receive, and the limits and besetments of mortality be forgotten and swallowed up in its fruition—the joys and glories of an endless immortality.

A WOMAN WITH A PURPOSE

PURPOSE ESSENTIAL TO SUCCESS—BIRTH AND PARENTAGE OF CAROLINA CORRADI—HER MOTHER'S PRESCIENCE—PREPARATION FOR FUTURE CAREER—DEVOTED WORK IN BEHALF OF DEAD KINDRED.

Few people have accomplished anything in this life worth mentioning who have not had a definite purpose in view, to which every faculty of their mind and body is made to bend. People without a purpose abound on every hand, with nothing in appearance to distinguish them from their fellows except a kind of mental or physical inertia or a fickleness of disposition, causing them to flit about from one pursuit to another, as a butterfly does from flower to flower. Their personal lack of purpose may not be apparent to the casual observer, especially if they be sufficiently under the influence of strong-minded, decisive friends, who furnish the purpose for them, and manipulate them as if they were human automatons.

Some people seem to be born with a purpose, or—more properly speaking—with a disposition to form a purpose, and adhere to it. They are not only possessed of energy, but of the power of concentration, the ability to apply themselves to the one particular purpose before them until they succeed.

Lacking a purpose—either innate or acquired—people are apt to drift aimlessly through life, like an abandoned boat upon the ocean, subject to every wind that blows and every current that flows. With conditions favorable, they may float on indefinitely, even as derelicts at sea have been known to do for years without meeting with any serious obstruction. Their course may be so serene, and so attended with good fortune, that observers may be almost forced to the conclusion that they have a charmed existence. The real test of their constancy and endurance comes to the mechanical derelicts when storms beset them and breakers loom up before them, and to their human prototypes when obstacles are encountered that only a strong mind can cope with, and when no friendly support is at hand, to lean upon. The weak and vacillating then flounder in uncertainty, so lacking in self-confidence as to be absolutely unable to formulate and execute any purposeful plan, while the strong-minded, resolute, self-reliant people carefully lay their plans, and then proceed to fulfill them.

Of course the majority of human derelicts are unwilling to admit that their failure to succeed is due to any fault of theirs. They prefer to believe that they are the victims of chance, or ill-luck, or lack of opportunity. Many of them have no desire to work, and others, if not really lazy, have no pride or interest in the work they do, and are therefore very indifferent workmen, and seldom retain a job long after getting it.

Occasionally a person is found who has sufficient mental grasp to devise, and executive ability to carry out a number of purposes simultaneously, and those who are specially successful in material affairs are sometimes called "Napoleons of finance." More frequently, however, the diffusion of energy due to following too many purposes results in failure. Many of the more conspicuous financial failures are made by persons who fairly bristle with purposes. They are like the ambitious but unwise blacksmith who had so many irons in the fire at once that he either had to slight his work on all or allow some to become overheated and spoiled.

It is infinitely more creditable to have one purpose, and accomplish it successfully, than a number and succeed only indifferently.

The story of which the foregoing is a prelude is not that of a "Napoleon of finance" or even of a Hetty Green in success in material matters, but of that of a very humble, but altogether worthy woman, whose aspirations are spiritual rather than material.

Examples from the ranks of the humble are more apt to be helpful to the great mass of the people than those taken from other classes, as what the wealthy and highly educated classes accomplish is apt to be attributed to their more favored station in life, and therefore not to be emulated by the poor, illiterate and obscure.

It will be observed that the example which follows is one that may be profitably emulated by any, regardless of rank in life.

Carolina Corradi was born September 1, 1856, in Mastetlen, Canton Thurgau, Switzerland. She was the youngest but one of eleven children, born of parents who were only in moderate circumstances, and therefore the help of all the children able to work was required to maintain the reputation for thrift which the family had always enjoyed.

The parents were honest, industrious, intelligent, but not specially pious people. Her father, Johannes Corradi, was a rather ingenious man, able to turn his hand to almost any kind of work, and as kind-hearted and self-sacrificing a man as could be found anywhere, and generous almost to a fault. He was greatly beloved by all who knew him, and especially by his children. The mother was an exceptionally good housekeeper, and possessed rare tact as a manager, and developed into quite a business woman, especially after her husband's death, when it became her duty to manage the material affairs of the family. She was also known by her intimates to possess a gift of prescience, or the ability to see things before they actually transpired. By this gift she evidently foresaw something of the future of her daughter Carolina while she was yet a young child, and insisted that she learn the French laundry business, as the time would come when she would find it an advantage to work at it. Carolina was the only child concerning whom the mother had this impression, although the other daughters were apparently as well adapted for that kind of work as she was, and there was nothing about her to indicate that she, any more than the others, would ever need to work at it. Like many other branches of knowledge or craft, the secrets of French laundry work were only to be obtained by sacrifice, and so the parents of Carolina paid a considerable sum of money for the privilege, and bound her to serve without pay for a certain period to have her learn from those who were skilled in that line.

She was apt at learning, became a very proficient hand, and followed that line of employment for about three years while her mother still lived, (her father having died when she was fourteen years of age.) The mother died in 1883, leaving the children, who, however, were all grown to maturity by that time, to shift for themselves. Her last words to Carolina were that she must not mourn or despair because of her death, as there was something great prepared for her, of which she was then in ignorance, but of which she would learn in due time. She said nothing of the kind about the other children, and the family talked about the fact after the mother's death and decided among themselves that it meant that Carolina was somehow going to become possessed of wealth. They had faith in their mother's ability to see things that were coming to pass, and they couldn't think of anything quite so desirable in their estimation as wealth.

Carolina went out to service, and was mostly engaged in general housework. While the parents lived the family never learned of the Gospel as taught by the Latter-day Saints, but some years later it was brought directly to the attention of some of the surviving members of the family, and Carolina alone of all of them was attracted by it. She joined the Church in the year 1889, and was so impressed with the doctrine of salvation for the dead, that she soon afterwards wrote a letter to the clerk of the parish in which her parents were born, to obtain information in regard to their ancestors. This was done in the hope that she might, at some time in the future, be able to have a vicarious work done in their behalf. To her gratification, the parish officer proved to be a distant relative, by the name of Corradi, and he supplied her with the names of her ancestors for a few generations—thirty-five or thirty-six names in all. They were all she was able to obtain, or knew where to obtain, before she migrated to Utah (which she did in the year 1891,) and she came here with a strong desire that they should have all the privileges of the Gospel that they might have enjoyed had they accepted of it in mortality.

She inherited enough from her parents' estate to pay for her emigration to Utah and leave $35.00 in her pocket when she landed here. That was the amount of her capital at the inception of her career here in Utah, less than twenty-three years ago. She had no relatives, and few acquaintances, in this land, and was unfamiliar with the language of the country.

She obtained work in a laundry at the lowest price paid to inexperienced hands, and was glad to get it. She was devoted to her religion, was faithful in attending meetings, paying her tithes and fast offerings, and never lost sight of the duty that she so early felt to be resting upon her, to do all that was in her power for the salvation of her dead kindred. In the meantime she had been acquiring a knowledge of the English language, but it was six years after she arrived in Utah before she began her vicarious work in the Temple. She was not able to follow this work up continuously—only to spend a day at a time, but the spirit of the work grew upon her. She was able to officiate for the females of her kindred, but she was in doubt as to how to proceed to get the work done for her male kindred. While in this state of anxiety the Spirit prompted her to apply to Niels P.L. Eskildz, with the assurance that he would faithfully serve, and be of great assistance to her. She accordingly applied to him, and, as already related, obtained his consent. When all those whose names she had were officiated for, she was favored with an open vision, in which a person appeared to her and told her that she had a great work yet to perform in behalf of her dead kindred—that she would do the work for more than a thousand.

At that time she did not know where she could get another name, and earned so little by her work (she never was paid more than $1.10 per day at the laundry, and much of the time only received

$1.00 per day) that she couldn't foresee how she could ever afford to pay for having her genealogy traced up and obtain more names. She had recently been trying to obtain laundry work (ironing) in private families, with a view to earning more than she had been able to at the laundries, but had not yet succeeded to any great extent. She felt, however, that the Lord had inspired the promise made to her, and that He could and would provide a way for its fulfillment, but how she could not forsee.

Soon afterwards she obtained work in her line in a private wealthy family, where she was able to earn $2.00 per day, and also learned of a man who was engaged in the business of tracing up genealogies, whom she employed to obtain the names of her ancestors. She has since obtained several extensive lists of names, including several lines of her ancestors, and has now had Brother Eskildz regularly employed for several years, whenever he has been able to do so, officiating for her dead male kindred, while she has employed women, and occasionally spends a day in the Temple herself, laboring for her female kindred. She has thus done herself, or hired others to do the work, for almost 1800, and by the time she completes the work for all the names she has, the number will be increased to fully 1900.

She has done this as a labor of love, and found great joy and satisfaction in so doing—in fact, feeling repaid as she has proceeded by the enjoyment the work has afforded her, for all the labor and sacrifice it has involved. While her earnings have never been munificent, she has maintained a decent, respectable appearance, keeping house in from one to three rented rooms, and honestly paid her way and done her duty as a church member—all from her own earnings.

She feels that the Lord has been specially kind to her, in providing a way for the gratification of her earnest desire in behalf of her dead kindred. She expresses also her gratitude to Brother Eskildz, to whom great credit is due for classifying the names and providing for the orderly and complete performance of the work, so that no names have been duplicated, and none omitted. She says she doesn't know how she could have accomplished what she has without his help. Her genealogical records are in fine shape, and are a credit to her.

When asked how much money she had spent for genealogical research, for books in which to keep a record of the work done and for the payment of people she had hired to officiate for her kindred, she replied she did not know, and she did not care to know. She was content to know that it had been spent in a worthy cause, gave the Lord the credit for it and did not even seek any personal recognition.

She has felt sure since embracing the Gospel that her mother must have had a foreknowledge that she would labor in this cause, and she has had many assurances since she first engaged in the Temple work that her parents are aware of the vicarious work she has done or caused to be done in behalf of the dead, and heartily approve of the same.

She has sought no notoriety in what she has done; in fact, was rather reluctant about admitting it or giving any information concerning it, but the consciousness of it affords her a great deal of satisfaction—infinitely more, she says that the possession of a million dollars could.

Some women have doubtless done more than she in laboring for the salvation of the dead, numbers considered, but her record offers a specially fine example of a holy purpose faithfully pursued, and Carolina Corradi will doubtless stand throughout eternity as the personification of self-sacrifice and filial devotion.

AN EXCEPTION

A RICH MAN'S HANDICAP—WEALTH NOT ESSENTIALLY BAD—BUT QUALITIES ITS POSSESSION DEVELOPS A BAR TO SALVATION—TYPICAL CASE OF A MAN REARED IN AFFLUENCE—UNPROMISING START IN MARRIED LIFE—HOW HE BECAME INTERESTED IN TEMPLE WORK—WORTHY EXAMPLE IN RECENT YEARS.

It is not an uncommon thing for a poor person to look with envy upon the possessions of the wealthy, and remark how easy it would be for him to be generous, and make sacrifices for a righteous cause, if he were only wealthy. It is hard—perhaps impossible—for such a person to realize it (never having been possessed of wealth,) but wealth is more frequently a bar to the service of the Lord than a help therein. We are informed in the gospel according to Matthew that the Savior said "a rich man shall hardly enter the kingdom of heaven;" and again, "it is easier for a camel to go through the eye of a needle than for a rich man to enter into the kingdom of heaven." Whether we understand from this that the Savior was indulging in hyperbole—the grossest kind of exaggeration, or that the eye of the needle referred to was a specially low gateway in the wall of Jerusalem, through which camels could only pass by crouching down, we must conclude that the rich are less susceptible to the saving influence of the Gospel than the poor. This is confirmed by the declaration that "Blessed are the poor in spirit, for theirs is the kingdom of heaven," and numerous passages about the deceitfulness of riches, and of "the love of money," being "the root of all evil."

When we come to analyze the question, it is not the wealth itself that is evil, but the avarice and arrogance that its possession is apt to develop, for the more one has the more he is apt to want. The person who in his youth is eager to acquire wealth is apt to grow intensely avaricious if not miserly in his old age. The person who

49

manifests pride and slight regard for others' rights in youth is apt to become unbearably arrogant as he grows older.

Humility is a pre-requisite to the acceptance and practice of those principles upon which salvation depends, and humility is the very opposite of arrogance. Treasures in heaven are apt to look most attractive to the person whose view thereof is not obstructed by treasures upon earth; for "where the treasure is, there will the heart be also." A poor person, seeking salvation, is not so apt to have his attention distracted therefrom, as is one who is full of care concerning his earthly possessions.

Inasmuch as the work done in the Temple is clearly in the nature of seeking treasures in heaven, it is really refreshing to find a wealthy person, and especially one who has been reared in affluence, manifesting much devotion in that line.

One of the most striking examples of this kind noticeable in the Salt Lake Temple in recent years is that of Brother P . . .

His parents were descended from aristocratic families of Old Virginia. His father was the owner of two large mercantile establishments and other valuable property in his native town before the war, but the war broke him up, and left him comparatively poor. However, he was of that class who cannot be kept down. He was ambitious and enterprising, and soon began to accumulate. Coming to Utah in the year 1864, he engaged in school teaching, farming, ran a threshing machine, clerked in, managed and then owned a store, engaged in banking, etc., wringing success out of everything he turned his hand to. By the time the subject if this sketch (who was born in Utah,) was old enough to receive impressions, his was regarded as among the most wealthy, influential and aggressive families in the state.

None of the sons (of whom there were several in the family) ever served as a missionary, until recently, when one of the younger sons filled a creditable mission to Germany. This fact is mentioned because the calling of one son from a household to fill a mission frequently arouses more or less zeal in the whole family.

Nor were they conspicuous workers in the quorum and auxiliary organizations in the church. This fact is mentioned for the same reason. When young people take an active part in these organizations they frequently develop into enthusiastic church members, and occasionally arouse an interest in spiritual matters throughout the whole family.

The eldest son was a successful mining broker, and prominent in political and business affairs, and the second, (the subject of this sketch) studied law, with the intention of becoming a practicing attorney. These facts are mentioned also for the reason that they are generally understood to tend from rather than towards religious devotion.

Another circumstance that would rather indicate backsliding than a growing zeal, was his disregard for the scriptural injunction: "Be ye not unequally yoked together with unbelievers." He married a girl who was not a member of the Church.

In extenuation, it may be said that he indulged in the hope of converting her; in fact, during the days of their courtship they read and discussed "Mormon" literature together, and she manifested an interest therein; but she hadn't faith enough to join the Church before her marriage; nor, indeed, for four years afterwards, the fact of her parents and most of her relatives being non-"Mormons" possibly accounting for her hesitancy.

With this introduction the story may now be given as told by Brother P..., of how he became interested in Temple work:

"On July 20, 1908, Miss H . . . and I were married by an Elder of the Church. Four years later my wife was stricken with hemorrhage of the brain, and her life was despaired of. She was healed in answer to prayer, and the faith exercised by herself and others, and gladly joined the Church soon afterwards. Later on, she was dying of organic Brights disease, and the physician in attendance said there was no possibility of her living. However, after an administration of the Elders, she improved immediately, and lived in peace for four years longer. On April 27, 1908, she died.

"We had not been to the Temple to receive our endowments, and to have the important ceremony performed whereby we could be united for time and all eternity.

"About one month after my wife's death I was impressed to go to the 20th Ward sacrament service; although I did not live in that ward, and it was my first attendance at a meeting there. Brother Samuel W. Jenkinson, a blind man, who was a Temple worker, was the speaker. Twelve years prior to that time Brother Jenkinson had done endowment work in the Temple for some of my wife's relatives, but he and I were not acquainted. I was so much impressed with his remarks, that I inquired and learned his name, and the following morning wrote a letter to this blind brother, telling him how pleased I was with his testimony.

"On receiving the letter, Brother Jenkinson telephoned to me a request to come up and see him. My telephone number was 5279.

"A month passed. One afternoon, on the very day the Temple closed for the summer vacation, as I was sitting at my desk, the telephone rang. Taking down the receiver, I heard the voice of Samuel W. Jenkinson, saying `Your telephone number has been coming to me for a week, especially while I was in the Temple. I did not call you up, as I did not wish to disturb you; but today the number '5279, 5279' came to me so many times that, on leaving the Temple, I have come to a phone. Now I do not know what to say to you.'

"That evening I called at the home of the blind brother, and talked to him awhile, mainly in regard to my departed wife.

"Six weeks passed. Three days before the Temple opened, after the vacation, Brother Jenkinson telephoned to me, saying: 'I am impressed that your wife wants her Temple work done.'

"'All right,' I replied, 'I will see to it.'

"I called upon President Winder, the presiding officer of the Temple, and told him what had occurred. He advised that I wait until a year had passed after the death of my wife. This agreed with my feelings exactly, and I remarked, `I think so too, President Winder. Besides, I would rather take the rest of the year to prepare to enter the Temple.'

"Three days later President Winder sent for me, and, when I responded to the call, said: `I have taken that matter up with President Smith, and we have made an exception in your case; and you can now do the work for your wife any time.'

"I thanked President Winder, but added that I thought there was no hurry, and preferred to wait for awhile.

"However, my wife knew the great importance of attending to this most sacred work without delay. In her life her rule was, not to procrastinate. She used to say, 'Tomorrow has enough duties of its own to attend to. So don't crowd the duties of today on tomorrow.' Besides, being in the spirit world, she had a livelier appreciation of Temple work than I had, with my earthly environment. She knew there was great danger in delaying to do the vicarious work—a fact that all Latter-day Saints should understand who are familiar with the teachings of the Prophet Joseph Smith upon the subject. He impressed upon the Saints in the strongest terms that there was none too much time left in which to do the work for the dead; and one of the strongest desires that he manifested during the last few weeks of his life was, that the Saints should proceed to get their genealogies and perform the sacred ordinances in behalf of their dead kindred without delay. Delays are dangerous, and the adversary will always give us abundant reasons for procrastination if we are willing to listen to such counsel.

"Ten days more passed. I was sitting at my desk when the telephone rang. Samuel W. Jenkinson's voice sounded in my ear; `You have let ten days go by, and haven't done that work for your wife yet.'

"My answer was: `No, I thought I would wait awhile; but I have permission from the First Presidency to do the work any time now.'

"Then came a short and vigorous sermon from the blind Temple worker, that has since proven to be the moving cause in my life in the matter of Temple work. Brother Jenkinson in plainness and earnestness said: 'I am impressed with the feeling that your wife wants her Temple work done, and I always act on my impressions. If her Temple work is done she will have more happiness and greater freedom, can progress faster and further, and can accomplish much more for herself and for others, and for you right here on earth. But you can do what you want. I hereby clear myself from all responsibility, and leave it wholly to you.'

"'I am convinced, Brother Jenkinson, and will see to it at once.' I answered, and took the next train for Ogden, where I saw my sister and asked her to be proxy for my wife.

"On seeing me, she exclaimed: 'I have been wanting to see you, and was going to write to you. I had a wonderful dream about your wife this morning.' She then proceeded to relate the dream, which was in line with my wife's wish, as expressed by Brother Jenkinson, that her Temple work should be done.

"Two days thereafter the Temple work was done, and it was the most glorious day of my life. No joy that I had previously felt could compare with the heavenly happiness that I experienced. Tears came to my eyes, and I rejoiced in a spirit of thanksgiving to my Heavenly Father for being permitted to enter His holy house and partake of the blessings therein bestowed.

"Since then I have felt that my main mission on earth is to have Temple work done for as many spirits as possible; thereby aiding in the release of those departed spirits from their prison houses. I have also taken the opportunity to encourage others to search out their genealogies and do Temple work for their kindred dead."

That is his story, briefly told. Others can testify to the fidelity with which he has fulfilled what he conceived to be his mission. He frequently goes to the Temple himself and receives ordinances in behalf of his dead kindred, and he is constantly employing others to do likewise, so that the work for his kindred dead goes on apace. Being asked how many he had now had the work done for, he replied that he did not know—he had not taken time to count—but some thousands.

In addition to all this, he has for the past five years been a worker on the Temple Block in connection with the Bureau of Information, spending much of his time there, and with good effect if the volunteered opinion of hundreds who have listened to him are a fair criterion by which to judge. Though he never filled a foreign mission, he has enjoyed privileges that seldom come to foreign missionaries. He has explained "Mormon" history and doctrine and borne his testimony to thousands who, as strangers thereto, were seeking the information he had to offer (and many of them willing listeners,) and who could never afterwards deny having heard the truth.

It may be inferred from this that he is working under high pressure, to spare so much time from his own absorbing affairs to devote to this charitable work, as well as to be under the financial tribute that he is in this connection, and indeed he is. He probably inherits from his father (who was a man of unusual energy, mental and physical,) his capacity for work. There is no doubt about his feeling better for the strenuous life that he is leading, and especially for his gratuitous work. He has been heard to remark that he has found no good and safe place to stop at, as any lessening of his efforts in the voluntary work for the good of others that he has undertaken, results in a perceptible diminution in the good spirit that he has enjoyed in recent years, and in his growing worldly-minded in a corresponding degree. His is a nature that is not satisfied with anything mediocre. He craves the best, and is naturally thorough and whole-hearted in that which he does, and has a keen sense of both enjoyment and suffering.

He has learned what many others fail to learn: that happiness depends less upon what we receive than what we give, less upon what we have than upon what we do; less upon what others do for us than upon what we do for them; and that we can adopt no more certain means of securing happiness for ourselves than that of seeking to make others happy. Life never was so full and rich and satisfying to him before as it has been in recent years, for he never did so much for others, and never before exhibited so much unselfishness.

He objects to being classed as a rich man, because, notwithstanding his interests are rather extensive, he has invested a large amount of borrowed money in an industry which involves a good deal of risk, and yet, with good fortune in his favor, may yield a handsome profit.

Well, if he is not rich he is certainly enterprising, and deserves to be rich, and never was in less danger from being rich.

Wealth is a comparative term, anyhow. If he is not rich compared with some who are very wealthy, he is compared with those who have little or none of this world's goods.

If, with the risk he is taking, he still finds time to devote so much unselfish attention to others, dead and living, how much more creditable than if he labored for selfish ends! And how much more of a sacrifice he is making than if he had converted all his surplus property into government bonds, the income from which would insure him a living without care on his part, and then only gave his time to the cause of humanity.

He has again married—this time in God's own appointed way, to one who is full of faith—and two lovely children have come to grace his home—the first living children he has had. He takes an optimistic view of life, and never felt that he had so much to live for.

It may be appropriately mentioned here that six years before his former wife died (a. already related,) she wrote a letter to her husband, with a request that it be opened and read after her death. His present wife chanced to read that letter some time after her marriage, and learned from it that the expressed desire of the deceased wife was that her husband should marry again, and that some time there would be a little Luacine (that being the first wife's name.) The first child was a boy. The second was a girl, and the mother, on her own volition, chose for her the name of Luacine.

Consider this case from whatever angle we may, Brother P . . . is an exception in his class, and a most praiseworthy exception, whose example in recent years is well worthy of emulation.

MY MOTHER

CHAPTER I

PREDICTION FROM MALACHI FULFILLED—BIRTH AND CHILDHOOD OF MARY ALICE CANNON—CANNON FAMILY EMBRACE THE GOSPEL—MIGRATE—MOTHER'S DEATH AT SEA—ARRIVAL AT NAUVOO—FATHER'S DEATH—HER MARRIAGE.

"Behold, I will send you Elijah the prophet before the coming of the great and dreadful day of the Lord, and he shall turn the heart of the fathers to the children, and the heart of the children to their fathers, lest I come and smite the earth with a curse."

Thus spake the Lord through Malachi, the prophet; but just what was meant by turning the heart of the fathers to the children and the heart of the children to the fathers, has been a matter of speculation among bible students since time was young. Of course, many have supposed that this prediction was fulfilled in the coming of John the Baptist; but wherein John the Baptist accomplished any such work as that indicated is not clear. Whatever the work was that Elijah was to do, there must be something potential about it, to have the effect of appeasing the wrath of the Almighty and averting the curse with which the earth (or possibly the inhabitants of the earth) would otherwise be smitten.

Not until the doctrine of salvation for the dead had been revealed was the full import of the declaration quoted from Malachi understood even by the Latter-day Saints. The anxiety they immediately experienced for the salvation of their kindred who had died without conforming to the Gospel requirements, when they learned that the living might do a vicarious work in behalf of the dead, that would place the latter upon an equal footing with the most favored of the living, was an illustration of its effects upon the children.

The interest that was awakened about that same time in the matter of genealogical research, without any apparent cause for it, more than had existed for ages, may reasonably be considered an evidence that the "heart of the fathers" was being turned to the children. Nor was this interest in the tracing of genealogies, and the connecting of one generation or age to another by kindred links, limited to Latter-day Saints, or those familiar with the doctrine of salvation for the dead, as newly revealed. It seemed to be a spontaneous feeling, specially noticeable in the more enlightened countries of that age and since. The disposition to engage in this research was not limited to any class or creed. It was manifested alike by people of various religious beliefs and by those also of infidel tendencies. Sometimes pride of ancestry furnished the excuse, and at other times the hope of inheritance was the incentive. Whatever the causes that led to the compiling and publishing of genealogical works, it is easy for Latter-day Saints to believe that men so actuated were inspired of the Lord, whether they realized it or not, and that the grand and ultimate purpose of the Lord was that the living believers in that doctrine might do a vicarious work for the salvation of individual dead, and thus connect the present generation with those of the past.

A desire to learn as much as possible about one's ancestors, and then go into the Temple and labor for their salvation, may be really accepted as the normal feeling among faithful, sincere Latter-day Saints. So generally is it understood to be their duty to labor for their dead kindred, that it seems quite the natural thing that they should do so. Their obligation in this respect is comparable to that of providing for dependent members of their households.

One must have a broader feeling of philanthropy or a higher sense of duty, to labor as a general worker or officiator in the Temple for extended periods, without hope of earthly reward. Among the more conspicuous examples of this kind in the Salt Lake Temple is Mrs. Mary Alice C. Lambert, the dean of the women workers, if such a term may be applied to a woman. She was one of those called to so labor when the Salt Lake Temple was completed, and has so served faithfully and gratuitously ever since, being still active and efficient, although in her eighty-sixth year. Hers is as fine an example of a busy, well-spent life, as could readily be found, and a perusal of the following sketch can hardly fail to be faith promoting:

On the 9th day of December, 1828, a young married couple, George and Ann Cannon, then living in the city of Liverpool, England, rejoiced in the birth of their second child—a daughter—whom they named Mary Alice. There was nothing about the child or her brother, George Q., who was two years her senior, or their parents, to distinguish them from the many thousands of other families who lived in that great city. The father was an intelligent and industrious tradesman—an expert carpenter, or joiner—and the mother a thoroughly domestic woman, whose love for her husband and children was only equalled by the strength of her religious fervor. Though England had been the adopted home of this branch of the Cannon family since many years before their marriage, the most of their relatives lived in the Isle of Man, and thither the family went on occasional visits. On one of these visits, at the earnest solicitation of her maternal grandmother, little Mary Alice was left to bear her company, and spent five years of her childhood in the quaint old town of Peel, for this purpose.

In course of time the Cannon family was enlarged by the successive births of other children—Ann, Angus, John, David and Leonora. John, however, died when three and a half years of age. Prosperity had attended the father's labors, the family had a comfortable and happy home, the older children were acquiring an education, and gave promise of being like other children among the better class in England—no worse than the majority, and not much if any better.

When Mary Alice was about 11 years of age, an event occurred that was destined to change the whole current of the family life. If there is any truth in the theory of heredity, it was well for the Cannon family that their ancestors, for generations, had been hardy seafaring men—some of them captains, conspicuous for their courage and adventurous disposition. It was well that their ancestral home was in the Isle of Man, where the inhabitants, largely fishermen, are inured to hardship and used to battling with the waves and braving the tempest. If any of the traits possessed by their ancestors had been inherited by the present generation, and especially strength of will and endurance, two of the most prominent characteristics of the Manx people—they must certainly be called into action in the strenuous life that lay before the Cannon family, thenceforward.

Some years previously Leonora Cannon, a sister of George Cannon, had migrated to Canada, and there met and married a young Englishman named John Taylor. Parley P. Pratt, as a Latter-day Saint missionary, soon afterwards visited the part of Canada where the Taylors lived, and they were converted and joined their fortunes with the Saints in Ohio. From Nauvoo John Taylor was sent on a mission to Great Britain, and immediately upon landing called upon his wife's brother and family.

A profound impression was made by this visit. The visitor had scarcely left the house, after a brief call, when the mother expressed the firm conviction she felt that he was a servant of God, although he had not then made known the fact that he was a missionary or explained the Gospel. After a very short time spent investigating the Gospel, the parents were baptized. Little Mary Alice, though so young, greatly desired baptism at the same time, but was too timid to ask for it. From the time she listened to the first conversation on the Gospel she had felt greatly exercised in regard to it, and earnestly prayed to the Lord for a testimony as to its truth. As a result, she obtained a strong assurance from the Lord of its truth, that has never since admitted of a doubt.

The parents had been members of the Church four months when, in June 1840, Elder Parley P. Pratt visited them in company with Elder Taylor. They had just finished eating breakfast, with the whole family present, when Elder Pratt, as if moved by a sudden inspiration, said: "Elder Taylor, have you preached the Gospel to these children? Some of them want to be baptized now. Don't you?" he asked looking straight at Mary Alice. "Yes, sir," she promptly replied, her heart so full of gratitude to the Lord for the opportunity she had prayed for of having her desire made known, that she could hardly speak. Further questioning resulted in immediate arrangements being made for the baptism of George Q., Mary Alice and Ann—all the children of the family then old enough for the ordinance.

It didn't take the family long to discover that there was no fellowship or tolerance for them among their relatives, or indeed among their former friends. Though formerly popular, they were now pitied or denounced, if not thoroughly hated. Whether this fact tended to create a desire to migrate to America or not, true it was that they soon obtained the spirit of gathering. The only social enjoyment the family found was in mingling with members of the church, and the desire soon grew strong to go where the majority of the members could be found. The mother especially revolted at the thought of her children growing up in an atmosphere of unbelief, and, although she was in delicate health, and had a premonition that amounted almost if not quite to an absolute fore-knowledge that she would not live to reach America, she insisted upon going, and was impatient to start. The father, too, after having a dream of his wife dying at sea, feared that it might prove true, and would have hesitated about going had the Lord not made known to him, in answer to prayer, that it was his duty to do so.

The family embarked on a sailing vessel bound for New Orleans in September, 1842, and the mother died and was buried at sea six weeks later, after suffering from sea sickness almost if not quite every day of the voyage up to that time. The forlorn condition of the family can more easily be imagined than described. The promises held out by the Gospel seemed to be their only comfort and support. For Mary Alice, mere child that she was, there was too much to do in caring for the younger brothers and sisters to admit of her yielding to grief. The new responsibility suddenly thrust upon her had the effect of merging her childhood into womanhood without any interim for youth.

The sea voyage ended at New Orleans, eight weeks after it commenced, the intention being to proceed immediately by river steamboat to Nauvoo; but obstacles were soon encountered, the first being the grounding of the boat on a sandbar, resulting in such a tedious delay that severe frost set in and the boat was unable to proceed farther north than St. Louis because of the river being frozen over. The Cannon family accordingly spent the winter in St. Louis, the father providing homes and support for two other families, whom he had charitably immigrated from England, besides his own.

Nauvoo was finally reached in April, 1843, seven months after the departure from England. A cordial greeting by the Prophet Joseph Smith and a hearty welcome from Aunt Leonora Taylor and family helped to reconcile them, and the peaceful home obtained in Nauvoo was all the more appreciated because of the difficulties experienced on the way.

In February, 1844, the father married a second time, the motherless condition of his children and a desire on his part for their welfare doubtless hastening the event.

This was a crucial period in the Church's history. Disaffection was rife, and the allegiance of many who had formerly been considered stalwarts in the faith had become very uncertain. Apostates, secret and outspoken, were conspiring with former enemies of the church to overthrow the work of the Lord and encompass the death of the Prophet. The martyrdom of the Prophet and Patriarch and the very serious wounding of Apostle John Taylor occurred, as a result of these diabolical plots, in June.

During all these trying times the Church had no more loyal

supporters than the Cannon family. The father was among those who cared for the bodies of the martyrs when returned to Nauvoo, and he it was who (with the assistance of his friend, Ariar Brower,) made the plaster casts of the faces and heads of the Prophet and Patriarch when the bodies were washed and prepared for burial.

In the August following, having gone to St. Louis to obtain employment, George Cannon suddenly died there. If the children's condition was forlorn when their mother died, it was doubly so now. The one fact, that they were located with the body of the Church, rendered their condition more tolerable. What might have been the result, so far as the children were concerned, of their being thus early left orphans if they had remained in England, can only be conjectured. The one supreme desire of the mother, to hasten the departure from England that the children might be with the body of the Church before being left without their natural protectors, was now justified.

George Q. and Ann found a home with their Aunt Leonora, the former, being already in the employ of Elder Taylor as a printer, and Mary Alice, though lacking two weeks of being sixteen years old at the time, married in November following, and provided a home for Angus, David and Leonora. Charles Lambert, the husband, was a thoroughly congenial companion, though twelve years the senior of his wife, and was willing as well as qualified to provide for the three orphans of whom he became the lawful guardian. He was an expert mechanic who, for the Gospel's sake, had given up a lucrative position and sacrificed worldly advantages in England to migrate to Nauvoo, where he landed in the early part of 1844. He had offered his services to help build the Temple without hope of payment therefor, and remained so employed up to the time the Temple was dedicated and he and his wife received their blessings therein, though his devotion thereto involved many hardships and severe privations, and almost superhuman self denial.

In all these trials Mother Lambert, as we now call her, and as she then was too, though not so called, (for her first child, Charles J., was born in Nauvoo in November, 1845, when she lacked one month of being 17 years old) was a true partner, patient, cheerful, industrious and self-sacrificing, and as loyal to the cause of God as the needle to the pole.

CHAPTER II

STRENUOUS LIFE IN NAUVOO—CITY BESIEGED— THRILLING EXPERIENCE—MIRACLE OF QUAILS—RUN OVER BY WAGON—WAGON SINKS TO BOTTOM OF RIVER—LIFE IN UTAH—MISSION ABROAD—HER POSTERITY.

They succeeded in acquiring a fairly comfortable home in Nauvoo, and a farm a short distance outside of the city, but they were not destined to long enjoy their possessions. The enemies of the Church were not content with having killed the Prophet and Patriarch; they were determined to drive the Saints from the state of Illinois, as they had previously been driven from Missouri. The Saints, especially in the outlying settlements, were continually being harassed by the lawless mob. Farms were frequently pillaged or their crops burned. Domestic animals were driven off, and the inhabitants in some instances severely beaten and compelled to flee from their homes to save their lives. Many of their houses were also set fire to before the owners' sight.

Not only were the Saints the victims of these ruthless depredations, but they were actually accused of being the perpetrators of the same, and this made the pretext by the mob for demanding that the Saints remove from the state or abandon their religion. Is it any wonder that some of the more weak and faithless of the members chose the latter alternative?

An agreement was finally entered into, between the Saints on one side, and state officials and leaders of the mob on the other, that the Saints should leave the state as soon as they could sell their possessions. It soon became apparent, however, that they would have to abandon their homes instead of selling them, as their enemies, though anxious to secure them, showed little disposition to pay for them.

The majority of the Saints living in Nauvoo left there to journey westward in the early part of the year 1846, leaving those whose services to work upon the Temple were required, or who lacked the necessary equipment for the journey, to follow on afterwards. When the Apostles returned later to Nauvoo to dedicate the Temple they exacted a promise from those yet remaining there, and who possessed the necessary outfits to undertake the journey, that they would not abandon any of the less fortunate Saints who might desire to accompany them, but help them out of the state. Before they were ready to depart, however, the mobocrats, in far superior numbers, surrounded and besieged the city.

Charles Lambert took a prominent part in the city's defense, helping to manipulate one of the cannons, which, in the emergency, he and others had improvised from an old steamboat shaft, and which had been mounted upon a part of the running gear of a wagon.

Mother Lambert was an interested and anxious spectator of the battle. In addition to having her own small family to care for, a Mrs. Haines, a neighbor, who was very ill, had been brought to her home to be nursed, her husband being absent from the city. During the bombardment, which continued for several days, some of the cannon balls fired by the mob passed close by, but none of them actually struck the house. In one instance an old gentleman, who felt too feeble to be among the city's defenders, but whose anxiety to see how the battle waged led him to ascend to the top of the roof of the Lambert house to get a good view, was so alarmed by a cannon ball passing close by his head, that he rolled from the roof to the ground.

A flag of truce was finally raised by the mob and a treaty effected, one of the provisions of which was that the Saints would vacate the city within three days. Such of the household goods possessed by the Lambert family as could be, were loaded into a wagon box and an attempt made to remove across the river. As they approached the Mississippi, however, in the lower part of the town, so many other wagons were found to be ahead of theirs, waiting to be ferried over, that a temporary camp was made near an abandoned home.

While on the way from their home to this point the family had been surrounded by a large posse of the mob and compelled to give up to them such fire arms as they possessed. Soon after reaching the temporary camp, and while Father Lambert was absent with his team for the purpose of hauling John Haines' wagon, with his household goods and his sick wife in it, down to the same point, a second mob appeared and demanded that Mother Lambert give up to them whatever fire arms were in the wagon. In vain she told them the weapons had already been surrendered, and that she did not have the keys to unlock the boxes in the wagon. They used a hammer to forcibly break open the boxes, and proceeded to ransack all that the wagon contained, with the result that they obtained possession of a sword and bowie knife. These they brandished before the frightened mother and panic-stricken children, accusing her of lying to them when she said she had no fire arms, and threatening to cut her head off.

A sister of the Prophet Joseph Smith was a witness of this scene, she having proffered to remain with Mother Lambert for company while her husband was absent, and expressed regret that she didn't have some weapon to shoot the men with while threatening her friend.

In course of time they succeeded in getting ferried over the river and formed a camp on the Iowa side until Father Lambert could fulfill his pledge to help the poor Saints who had no means of conveyance, across the river, where they would be free from the power of the mob.

While engaged in this mission of charity, a party of mobocrats recognized him as one who had been conspicuous in the fight, and, with guns aimed at him, ordered his surrender. Then, while the two largest men of the party took him down into the the river and held him under the water three times in succession until his breath was gone, fourteen others, with their guns cocked and ready for action, threatened to shoot him if he attempted to resist.

Of course, he did not resist, neither did two brethren who were with him at the time—Thomas Harrington and Daniel Hill—for they were unarmed and knew it would be folly to do so. They were silent witnesses of the scene, and neither they nor Father Lambert made any response to the oaths of their persecutors, nor to the threat that if they ventured upon that side of the river again they would be shot on sight. Notwithstanding the threat, however, Father Lambert was in Nauvoo the following day, and continued to go over there until all the poor Saints who cared to be helped across the river had abandoned the city.

On one of these occasions he was detained in Nauvoo, because of the pressing nature of what he had in hand, and Mother Lambert, fearing the mob had caught him and executed their threat, walked the bank of the river all night in the greatest agony of suspense, and inquired anxiously about her husband of every passenger that crossed on the ferry boat, but all in vain. However, he showed up the next morning, with an additional yoke of cattle which he had secured on an account due him.

While encamped on the bank of the river on the Iowa side, a rain storm occurred, which continued without cessation for three days and nights, until the wagons and their contents, as well as the clothing worn, were thoroughly soaked. The sick woman, Mrs. Haines, was placed on a bed under the wagon, that being the most sheltered place available, and there Mother Lambert and others waited upon her as best they could, even holding milk pans over her bed to catch the water as it dripped through the wagon box, until she died—a martyr to the persecution to which the Saints were subjected.

It was while encamped on the bank of this river that the Saints, many of them suffering for want of food as well as otherwise ailing, were visited by a flock of quails, miraculously rendered so tame that some of them alighted on the beds occupied by the sick and were caught by their hands, and others allowed themselves to be killed with sticks. Those persecuted and suffering Saints, the Lambert family among the rest, accepted the birds as sent of the Lord, considering themselves as much the objects of divine favor as were the Israelites of old when fed with manna, and cooked the quail and ate them with the greatest possible relish.

The journey through Iowa was a very difficult one, and not entirely devoid of danger. The country was very sparsely settled, there were no really good roads except occasional stretches of natural prairie, and the numerous streams encountered generally had to be forded because of the absence of bridges. However, they did not travel continuously, a stop of some weeks being made at Bonaparte, and employment obtained by which supplies were earned.

It was while traveling westward from that point that a very serious accident occurred. Mother Lambert was very nervous about riding over bad places, preferring to walk when allowed to do so. The fact that the team animals, which consisted of two yoke of steers and one yoke of cows, were not well broken—in fact, quite wild when they left Nauvoo—rendered her more chary about riding. When approaching Soap Creek, which she had learned was a difficult stream to cross, she alighted from the wagon, and soon afterwards, by some accident, fell in front of the wagon wheel, and, before the team could be stopped, two wheels had passed over the small of her back. In addition to the weight of the wagon itself, its load amounted to fully 3500 pounds, making a combined weight sufficient to crush the life out of a person under ordinary circumstances. Indeed, it was supposed when she was picked up that she was dead. Father Lambert, however, was not willing to admit such a possibility, and called upon as many of his fellow travelers as had any faith to join with him in administering to her. His wife was miraculously spared, and the journey resumed the following day, but she has suffered more or less ever since from the effects of the accident.

Winter Quarters, on the west bank of the Missouri river, where the main body of the Saints had encamped, was reached late in November, and, as soon as Father Lambert had constructed a log house to shelter his family during the winter, he made his way to Missouri and found employment by which he earned supplies, and sent to his wife and children. He and his family were ambitious to journey westward with the pioneers in the spring. They were prevented, however, from doing so by the Indians killing their team animals after they had been brought through the winter in good condition, and shortly before the journey was to be undertaken.

It was a sad disappointment, but only a temporary set back. With courage unabated, the family removed to St. Joseph, Mo., where living was cheap and work abundant, and in February of the following year, with a new team and supplies earned in Missouri, Mother Lambert and the children were sent forward to Winter Quarters, to be ready to undertake the journey westward, while Father Lambert remained in Missouri to work as long as possible before rejoining them.

That journey of 150 miles in that inclement season was a terrible one, but it was bravely accomplished. In crossing the river from Ferry Point to Winter Quarters, however, a new misfortune occurred. The river had been frozen over for a considerable period, and teams had passed over it on the ice with impunity. Even that very morning two heavily loaded wagons had gone over. Yet, when the Lambert wagon was being taken across, although the precaution had been resorted to of taking the team over first and drawing the wagon over from a distance with a rope, the ice gave way. There, in that bleak March weather, six weeks before her son George was born, Mother Lambert stood upon the bank of the Missouri river, with her child in her arms and her two young brothers and younger sister clinging to her skirts, and saw the wagon containing all the family's earthly substance sink through the ice to the bottom of the stream. Sister Jane Dutson, (afterwards Mrs. Alexander Melville, of Fillmore) who had accompanied Mother Lambert from Missouri, stood beside her when the wagon disappeared, and the catastrophe almost made their hearts cease beating.

They never expected to see the wagon or its contents again. The accident, however, didn't prove so serious as that. The occasion served to illustrate how spontaneously kind, sympathetic and resourceful Latter-day Saints are. Though Mother Lambert had few acquaintances in Winter Quarters, the news of her misfortune soon spread, and proffers of help and expressions of sympathy came from all quarters. Volunteers soon plunged into the ice-cold water and readily reappeared bearing in their hands articles recovered from the wagon, which in turn were seized by others standing near the edge of the ice and then loaded upon hand sleds and conveyed to the shore. Before night set in most of the contents of the wagon had been recovered—damaged, of course, but not completely spoiled, and all done without any intimation of a favor being conferred thereby, much less any kind of remuneration being expected. Depend upon it, though, Mother Lambert was not lacking in gratitude, and in her prayers that night as she enjoyed the shelter of Brother Harrington's hospitable roof, she thanked God with all the fervency of which she was capable that she was a Latter-day Saint, and for the fraternal spirit that abounded among her fellow members.

The next day, by some method not now remembered, the wagon also was recovered.

Very soon afterwards President Young, who was then at Winter Quarters, preparing to start on his second trip to the Salt Lake

Valley, accompanied by his family, wrote to Father Lambert in Missouri, advising that he remain there another year, promising, as a condition of his doing so, that he should lose nothing, but be able to go with a much better outfit than he otherwise could. Mother Lambert and the children accordingly returned thither, and awaited the arrival of the spring of 1849.

The journey to the valley, which occupied six months, was full of vicissitudes and rich in the experience that tends most to develop character. The goal for which the family had longed and prayed, though a wild region, forbidding in appearance, was hailed with joy, as promising exemption from contact with a sinful world, and freedom from persecution.

One thing that was specially disappointing to Mother Lambert and her three proteges was, that their brother George Q., who, with his sister Ann had reached the valley in 1847, soon after the pioneers landed, had only the day before started on a mission to California, thence to proceed to the Sandwich Islands. This involved a separation, as it afterwards proved (counting from the time they parted in Winter Quarters,) of almost eight years. He had, in anticipation of the family's arrival, arranged for the purchase of a lot—the same lot which was the family's home for so many years, and still in their possession, and made some adobes from which they might construct a house.

As illustrative of Father Lambert's disposition to follow the counsel of the church leaders, it may here be mentioned that President Willard Richards, one of the pioneers, and second counselor to President Young, who entertained a very strong friendship for Father Lambert, had saved a corner lot on Main Street—that which Walker Bros. bank occupied for so many years—for his friend, and so informed him on his arrival. Father Lambert expressed his gratitude for the kindness, but said, as President Young's counsel was that no family should have more than one city lot, and his brother-in-law, George Q., had bargained for a lot for him a couple of blocks distant from Main Street (the price of which must be paid) and made some adobes with which to build thereon, he felt that he ought to decline Brother Richards' kind offer. One has only to recall the almost fabulous value of that Main Street lot at the present time to realize what he lost by that declination, and yet, if its possession would have made the family become worldly-minded and think less of their religion, Father Lambert must even now, if permitted to know anything of mundane affairs, thank God that he did not accept it.

Those early years in Salt Lake Valley were years of desperate toil, hardship and privation, of which the Lambert family had their full share—perhaps more than their share; not however, from want of effort on their part, for none were more industrious or frugal, but largely because of their willingness to help others.

A more generous man than Charles Lambert probably never lived. He found more pleasure in relieving the wants of others who were in need than self gratification ever could have afforded him, and his wife was a worthy partner in that same respect. The needy did not have to apply to them to obtain assistance; they were sought for and their wants relieved without ostentation. No family ever bore privation with less complaining. When the crops failed through the ravages of grasshoppers, weeks passed without even the children of the household and served first the were they and bread, tasting the last to go without.

No woman in Utah probably had the faculty of preparing for her family a more palatable meal from herbs and roots than Mother Lambert, nor more wholesome and enjoyable fare when food was more plentiful and varied. How she accomplished the herculean tasks which came to her, and which she performed uncomplainingly, is incomprehensible to the present generation. Her first three children being boys, and their services being otherwise required, she had very little help in the household the greater part of the time she was bearing children, and she was the mother of fourteen. (She didn't shirk the duties of motherhood.) She was the dressmaker and tailoress for the family, even to the carding and spinning of the wool some of the time. Hers also was the task of cooking for the family, and not with the present facilities either. The open fireplace with its bake kettle and skillet and frying pan, and the adobe oven, were her early culinary conveniences in Utah. These were succeeded by the sheet iron stove, and that by the cast iron stove, and so on up to the range. She did the butter making and washing and ironing and mending for the family too, and it was always a big family, frequently including hired male help. She was the housekeeper also, and a good housekeeper too, the house being seldom out of order. It presented a cheery welcome to friends and acquaintances from far and near, and many availed themselves of it.

Hers was no stinted hospitality. The best she had was at the disposal of all who called, and frequently even the floors were taxed to their capacity to find room for the beds of those she entertained.

She was a good disciplinarian too. All her children as they grew up were taught to work, and in turn bore their share of the burden. She was also a famous nurse, and possessed of considerable skill in the use of the simple remedies that served so well to maintain a standard of health that has not been equaled in more recent years, notwithstanding our numerous and high-priced doctors. In these latter respects her services were not limited to members of her own household by any means.

Her own health was never especially robust, though she must have inherited a strong constitution and possessed naturally an indomitable will. She was seldom free from pain in her back, as a result of the accident before mentioned. Her powers were taxed too, upon numerous occasions, and for extended periods, in caring for an ailing husband, although he was a man who would bear any amount of pain without complaint. He was a great sufferer from inflammatory rheumatism, which caused a partial loss or his eyesight several times, and for more than six months at one time he was without the use of one arm, through having his shoulder dislocated.

The death of her husband, which occurred more than twenty-two years since, added an additional burden to her, but it also called forth her self-reliance, and proved that she possessed considerable executive ability.

In addition to all the labors and cares and duties mentioned, Mother Lambert found time throughout a very large part of her career for a great deal of charity work. For fifteen and a half years she was secretary of the relief society of the 7th ward, and for the succeeding twenty-two years was its president. She filled the last named office up to the time she removed from the ward, and her removal was for the purpose of being near the Temple, having been called to be one of its regular workers at the time that edifice was completed in 1893.

She filled a mission to England with her husband in 1882-3 and spent several months visiting different countries in Europe in 1906, mainly for the purpose of obtaining genealogical data. She has performed ordinances in the Temple for hundreds of her relatives and friends who died without the privilege of accepting the Gospel. She has also labored to a considerable extent as a missionary from the general board of the Relief Society, her travels in this capacity extending from Idaho in the north to Mexico in the south.

As an indication of the devotion of Mother Lambert and her family to the cause of truth, it may be said that the missionary work performed by herself and direct progeny (including the general work in the Temple, by direct call of the Church authorities) amounts in the aggregate to more than fifty-eight years.

Hers has been an unusually busy and useful life, and, according to her opinion, a rather happy one. She feels that she has had more real joy during her eighty-five and a half years upon earth than usually falls to the lot of mortals. And why not? A faithful adherence to duty throughout her life has left her comparatively little to regret, and unhappiness is largely the result of regret and remorse for sins committed and opportunities lost. Happiness depends less upon worldly possessions and a life of ease than upon a pure heart and a clear conscience. Her present joy is all the more complete for the sorrow she has felt; the peace of her recent years all the more enjoyable for the trials and turmoil of the past, and the comfortable competence she now enjoys is all the more appreciated because of her early privations.

If happiness is at all dependent upon the love of kindred, she ought to be supremely happy; for she has a numerous posterity, who almost idolize her. She is not able to wholly gratify the wishes of her several sons and daughters, because of her inability to spend her remaining days in mortality as a member of the household of each; so until recently she maintained her own modest but comfortable home and enjoyed a hearty welcome at the home of any of them as often and as long as she chose to visit.

During recent years the infirmity of age has led her to give up housekeeping and take up her residence with her eldest daughter. She receives every attention that love and duty can suggest, and is happy and contented. She is still a model of industry, seldom being seated for many minutes without having some kind of needlework, writing or reading to give her attention to.

In this connection it may be mentioned that for a great many years past it has been her habit to exhibit specimens of her needle work produced during the previous year at the annual State Fair, and has always received recognition, and sometimes the highest prizes, for the excellence of her productions.

As an indication of her methodical habits, it may be mentioned that she keeps a diary, or journal, in which she daily records, with her own hand, passing events of local or general interest, and especially happenings among her own family or progeny, and her financial transactions, as well as how she spends her time and the condition of her health. This has been her daily practice ever since shortly after her husband's death, and is a continuation of the journal which he kept during the greater part of his life.

It may be mentioned that Mother Lambert's personal accidents during her later years have been somewhat numerous, mainly because of her independence and disposition to do things herself rather than ask anyone else to do them for her. She has suffered from broken ribs no less than six different times, but she has always rallied wonderfully quick from any injury or ailment.

She takes a great interest in all of her progeny, remembers their names and quite generally their birthdays, and frequently visits among them. Her children appreciate her wise counsel and motherly interest, and feel, one and all, that whatever of merit they have accomplished in life has been due to the inspiring example and wholesome precepts set before them by her and their revered father.

To him not less than to her do they feel indebted, and forever shall be though they become the best and most dutiful of sons and daughters, for he was a model father, as loving, kind, self-sacrificing, honest, industrious and faithful as mortal father ever was. He alone of all his father's family embraced the Gospel as revealed anew, but from him and Mother Lambert, through the blessing of the Lord, a direct progeny has resulted (including three generations) to the number of 201, all of whom are living except 29, and all in the faith for which he sacrificed so much, and which was his guiding star through life.

Scarcely less remarkable has been the increase from the Cannon family generally, although the posterity of Mother Lambert outnumbers those of any one of her brothers or sisters. The direct descendants of George Cannon (including the six children already mentioned as having been left orphans, and their sister Elizabeth, born as a product of the second marriage six months after her father's death) who are living number almost 700, to say nothing of those who have died. In view of the fact that their numerous relatives left in England and the Isle of Man have actually decreased until their known descendents scarcely outnumber the fingers on one's two hands, we may well exclaim, "What hath God wrought!"

EXAMPLES OF RIGHTEOUS ZEAL

NIGHT WORKERS WHO SERVE IN THE TEMPLE DURING THE DAY—MANY WOMEN SERVE AT GREAT PERSONAL SACRIFICE—TEMPLE WORK A BOON TO THE BLIND.

Among those who are in daily attendance at the Salt Lake Temple, officiating for the dead, are quite a number of men who are deserving of special credit, because of the personal sacrifice the service involves. Allusion is made to those who earn their living by working at night, and then deny themselves the sleep and rest their tired natures crave, by devoting a good half day's service to Temple work, either for their own kindred dead or others. Indeed, it occasionally amounts to considerably more than half a day. They usually form part of the morning company, all the members of which are supposed to be present and seated before 9 a. m., when the introductory service commences. Under ordinary conditions, they may expect to emerge from the Temple about two o'clock; but if the company be unusually large, (as it is quite frequently,) it may be nearer 4 p. m. before they get out.

Most men object strongly to being deprived of ample and regular hours of rest and sleep, and many persons would rather make a financial sacrifice than forego the sleep and rest they feel that they require.

If they had to work all night they would feel that any kind of service during the day, to which they would have to give strict attention for several successive hours, would be absolutely out of the question.

The examples in mind are men in humble or moderate circumstances, who possibly couldn't very well afford to hire others to officiate for them; so if they failed to do it themselves, by sheer self denial, it would probably not be done.

August Roth is employed at the car barn in this city, cleaning out cars (which is very tiresome work,) from 6 p. m. to 6. a. m., every night in the week, yet is almost invariably at the Temple two days a week, and sometimes three. He and his wife (and a lady friend who occasionally comes with them) have, during the past six years, done the work for about 800 persons, mostly his or his wife's relatives. For a poor man, he has also been very generous in his free will offerings to the Temple. It has been his habit to contribute fifty cents every time he comes to the Temple.

Karl Niemelka has also been employed at the car barn at night for several years past, and done a good deal of work in the Temple (though not as much as Brother Roth) for his dead kindred, and has just left to fill a mission to his native land. While absent he hopes to engage in genealogical research, and be the better prepared for Temple work on his return.

John C. Hoggan is employed as a nightwatchman, having the care of a large amount of business property, and is required to be on duty and generally moving about from 8 p. m. until 6:15 a. m. every night in the week. Notwithstanding this, he has averaged fully two days a week at the Temple for the past eight years, working mostly for his own and his wife's kindred, but occasionally for others, and all that he has received for his service in behalf of others he has contributed to the missionary fund, in the ward in which he resides.

Albert A. Quellmalz is janitor in a large office building and a number of stores, to which he has to devote eight hours work between the time business closes at night and opens in the morning. Yet he never fails to serve in the Temple on Tuesday, the day devoted to baptisms, as well as the three succeeding days of the week. He has during the past eight years officiated for about 650 dead relatives and friends. Brother Quellmalz is a very studious, methodical man, and enjoys quite a reputation for efficient service in other capacities in the Church.

John N. Swift is employed as a janitor by one of the railway companies every night in the week, being on duty from 5 p. m. until 8 a. m. In addition to this, he has served regularly in the Temple during the past six years on Thursday and Friday. Some indication of the sacrifice this service involves is conveyed in the statement that, although his home is in Sugar House Ward, not a great distance away, he is necessarily absent therefrom continuously from Wednesday at 4:30 p. m. until Saturday at 9 a. m. His service in the Temple has been entirely in the interest of his own relatives.

John S. Muir has been employed by the Church for twenty years past as nightwatchman, formerly at the tithing office and yards, but since its erection at the Bishop's Building, every night in the week. During the past twelve years he has spent from one to two days a week in the Temple, having done the work for rather more than 600 persons.

Jedediah M. Brown, of South Bountiful, has been janitor at the large public school building in that region for the past twenty years, and during six years of that time was also nightwatchman at the Deseret Live Stock Co. Store. Yet during all that period, with the exception of fourteen months while he was absent on a mission, he has spent on an average two days a week in the Temple. For a number of years past his health has been quite poor, having contracted chills and fever while on his mission, which later developed into chronic rheumatism, from which he has suffered ever since. Whatever the condition of his health, however, he has never yet felt willing to give up his service in behalf of the dead. In addition to the service mentioned, he is under the necessity of traveling about twenty miles by train or otherwise every day he serves in the Temple.

Ernest R. S. Schnelle is also employed as a nightwatchman, in an outlying business district, and is responsible for a great deal of valuable property, some of which tramps are specially liable to prey upon, so that he has to be constantly wide awake and alert for twelve hours at a stretch every night, but he is among the most regular and devoted of the Temple workers.

Robert Hunter, who is nightwatchman at Z. C. M. I., is a frequent attendant at the Temple, mostly laboring for others, because of lacking names of his own kindred dead, and is in the habit of voluntarily contributing to the Temple expense fund all that he receives for his service.

Doubtless many of the women who are in daily attendance at the Temple, so serve at very great personal sacrifice. Self denying women seldom expect or receive full credit in this life for what they do in the way of service. Perhaps only the All-seeing Father or recording angels know all of the heroism involved in the nightly toil and rigid self-denial with which many, possibly most, of the sisters patiently and uncomplainingly serve in the Temple for the benefit of those who are powerless to repay them in this life. It would be difficult to find a more devoted and truly charitable class of women than those laboring in the Salt Lake Temple.

The women in attendance at the Temple almost invariably far outnumber the men—sometimes two to one. Another characteristic of the regular attendants is that there is a preponderance of foreigners. A very large proportion of the regular workers are Scandinavians. The Swiss and Germans are also quite largely represented.

One of the most self-denying and devoted women who ever served in the Salt Lake Temple was Sister Berger, or (as she was known in the Temple, by the name of her first husband) Catherina B. Moosheer. She was a native of Zurich, Switzerland, being born January 25, 1823. From the time she embraced the Gospel she was very much concerned about the salvation of her dead kindred, and took care to obtain all the information possible about her ancestors.

She arrived in Utah July 4, 1872, accompanied by her son and daughter. She purchased a home and exerted herself to the utmost to make her own way in the world by engaging as a nurse, by which she accumulated considerable property. She had the work done for her immediate ancestors as early as 1876, in the Endowment House. After that she found an opportunity of having her genealogy traced up by a party who was engaged in that line, and spent money very freely for that purpose. She worked in the Temple almost from the time it opened. In 1895 she was partially paralyzed, and never fully recovered therefrom. This made her if possible more anxious than ever to hasten the work for her dead kindred. She sold her home to obtain the means necessary to secure as many names as possible of her dead kindred, and to employ men and women to help her in doing the work for them. Her records show that in all sixty-five different people were employed to assist her. For a period of two and a half years she had twelve persons—six men and six women—constantly employed in helping her in the Temple. She had the work fully done for 1,748 of her dead kindred, and sacrificed all that she possessed in order to accomplish it.

It may be of interest to note that Sister Moosheer was the first Temple worker to complete a record of 1,000 names.

She died in Salt Lake City June 9, 1899, shortly after completing the work for the last name she had of her dead kindred.

Her son and daughter and their families gave her every possible encouragement in the Temple work while she lived, and are now more proud of what she accomplished therein than they would be if she had left them fortunes.

Another very devoted woman in the Temple work is Sister Catherina Z. Schuler. She is also a native of Switzerland, having been born in Glarus, May 22, 1834. She not only sacrificed her home there for the Gospel's sake, but left her husband also because of his determined opposition to her religion.

Bringing her son with her, she came to Utah and located first at Logan, where she remained for several years, and where her son subsequently died. She was present at the dedication of the Logan

Temple, and did a good deal of work there for her dead kindred, of whom she had or subsequently obtained a very extensive list.

She removed to Salt Lake City in 1892, and witnessed also the dedication of the Temple in this city. She was dependent entirely upon her own earnings, and went out sewing as she found opportunity, and did Temple work occasionally. Since 1898 she has devoted herself exclusively to her Temple work, in which she has been assisted by many friends, and devoted every cent she could save to hiring men to work for her male kindred. In all, she has done, or had done, the work for fully 2,400 of her kindred dead.

A look at Sister Schuler's face is sufficient to convince any person that hers is a joyful work. Though she is now past eighty years of age, and has always been used to hard work, she is well preserved and active, and, though not mirthful, she is ever good natured, patient and contented. As in the case of many others who are active in Temple work, that labor has doubtless added years to her life, and rendered her declining days in mortality about the happiest she has ever spent. The consciousness of being a savior of others has brought her more joy than the possession of wealth or worldly honors ever could.

Sister Annie Davis Watson, widow of the late Joseph M. Watson, was a worker in the Temple for seventeen years, and only gave up the work because of her hearing growing so bad that she could not continue. Her husband died in the year 1895. She never had any children, and her life would have been extremely lonely if she had not interested herself in the work for the dead. She had a desire to devote herself to working for her husband's dead kindred, and mentioned the matter to President Snow, telling him if she could not so labor she had no desire to live; also that she had no genealogy of her husband's kindred farther back than his parents, for whom the work had already been done. He told her she would be able to obtain the genealogical information necessary, advised her to take up the work and promised there should be no end to it. He also told her that her husband in the spirit world would be familiar with every circumstance connected with the work as it progressed.

She has since devoted her life and her income to the work, and either officiated herself, or employed others to officiate, for 15,247 dead persons, most of whom are her husband's kindred.

She says it is the most glorious work she ever engaged in, and she has felt the presence of her husband's spirit upon many occasions.

There is one special class to whom the vicarious work in the Salt Lake Temple must be a very great boon. The blind, of whom there are quite a number of both sexes, in daily attendance, seem to find special comfort in the work. The opportunities people have of making themselves useful to their fellows, after being deprived of the priceless gift of sight, are extremely limited. People of independent minds dislike to be always treated as objects of charity. They like to feel that they are of some use in the world, and it is doubtful if there is any other work in which the average blind person can engage with so much satisfaction as that in the Temple. It is usually conceded that the loss of sight by a normal person has the effect of quickening and strengthening his remaining senses, and it is quite possible that the most of the sightless workers in the Temple get more enjoyment out of the work than the average person who retains his sight. He is perhaps able to think more profoundly, and is more susceptible to the impressions of the Spirit than if he had the use of his eyes.

Perhaps no man that ever labored in the Temple enjoyed the Spirit of the work more and shed a better influence among his associates than did Samuel W. Jenkinson, a blind brother of rather unusual intelligence and devotion, who died about three years since, and of whose experiences more may be said hereafter.